# BLOODY YORKSHIRE

## Volume 2

**W M Rhodes**

# Copyright

La di Dah Publishing
Royal Crescent Court
Filey
North Yorkshire YO14 9JH

First Published 2020

**FIRST EDITION**



Source. ISBN: 978-1-8381769-07

# DEDICATION

Truth will come to sight, murder cannot be hid for long.
William  Shakespeare


# FOR THE VICTIMS

'Let us hope their souls are happy in heaven among the best.
While their murderer's do remain on earth deprived of their rest.'

# CONTENTS

# ACKNOWLEDGMENTS

To all victims of crime past and present, and to their families who must suffer the consequences

The stories reconstructed in this book are from actual events.
The information therein, and the crimes depicted, are based on legal
evidence, statements, eyewitness accounts, court transcripts, newspapers
and testimony given by those involved, personal interviews, individual
research, and media resources.

# INTRODUCTION

## York Executions

*York Castle 1644. By W. H. Toms*
*(18th-century engraver), 1911, Public Domain.*

For centuries York was the centre for administering justice for the criminally convicted of Yorkshire. Punishments were bloody and often gruesome.

On 1st March 1379, bailiffs of the city and county of York with magistrates and eminent gentleman met to consider and agree on erecting new gallows to replace the gibbet post, which the city used for hangings for many years.

## TYBURN 'THE THREE-LEGGED MARE.'

*The Three-Legged Mare. York Museums Trust. Public Domain*

The bailiffs agreed to dismantle the old gibbet and erect new gallows in the area known as Knavesmire, on the south side opposite York Moor, about a mile from York Castle. The project completed in March 1379 and named York Tyburn after the London gallows at Marble Arch. However, because of their triangular structure, three beams supported by three uprights, the gallows were nicknamed the three-legged mare. These gallows used the 'short drop' method of execution, which means the hangman left their victims to die by slow strangulation.

The first man to be executed at the new three-legged mare was Edward Hewison for rape on 31st March 1379. Coincidentally over four hundred years later 29th August 1801, Edward Hughes, a private soldier with the 18th Light Dragoons, is recorded as the last man executed at the Tyburn three-legged mare, and like Hewison on a conviction of rape. The public believed in Hughes innocence, a public outcry erupted, and a grace period of fourteen days agreed. However, his appeal was unsuccessful, and any request for mercy rejected. The authorities considered the crime so atrocious, made worse by the circumstances of Hughes' military profession, which aggravated matters. They committed him to York Castle on the sworn oath of Mary Brown of Tollerton, who said Hughes had ravished her, and he knew of her body without her consent in a field in Easingwold.

Besides Tyburn, gallows existed in York at various church institutions, and they each had their separate individual systems of justice. The Abbot of St Mary's governed, Burton Stone Lane. The Dean & Chapter of York controlled another at the junction of Haxby Road and Wiggington Road. St Leonard's presided over the gallows at Green Dykes without the Bar. The Archbishop of York owned gallows in Fossgate. At that time, the church hanged more people than the Crown did.

On 3rd June 1700, the Grand Jury petitioned the judges at the Lent March Assizes to remove the old gallows belonging to St Leonard. It gave great joy to the citizens of York when the Home Secretary agreed to these proposals and dismantled these unsightly gallows. Leonard Gaskill and Peter Rook were executed for sheep-stealing, became the last two victims to suffer the extreme penalty of the law on these gallows in 1676.

Eventually, the people of York objected to Tyburn because of its proximity to the entrance of the historic city. Changing attitudes meant residents considered the impression visitors received of the town – whose first sight was the town's gallows – to be too daunting. Furthermore, they felt the lengthy journey from the castle to the place of execution too gruelling and far too inhumane for the condemned convict. The sentiment was that the '*entrance to the town should no longer be annoyed by dragging criminals through the streets.* (The History of York) The York's Herald newspaper explained its relocation on 25th July 1800, as follows: '*Thus will be removed from one of the principal roads leading to the city that disagreeable nuisance, the gallows; and thus, will the inhabitants and passengers be no longer interrupted, and their humanity hurt, by  the leading of unfortunate people to the place of execution.*' The Tyburn gallows stood unused for a further 11 years and finally dismantled in 1812.

*A plaque in remembrance of the hanging site of York Tyburn*

From 1801, the Crown Justice administered justice at York Castle for executions in Yorkshire. Huge crowds would gather to watch convicts – from murderers to petty thieves to witness the final fate of a condemned criminal. In part, people were encouraged to attend them because the authorities felt that the harsh public execution would deter them from committing a crime. People would cheer as they watched the convicted put into carts sitting next to their coffins, with a  noose around their necks as they began their final journey. Biographies of the convicted were reported in the press who would relish on the crimes – often sold in Broadsheets or recited in poetry or a ballad.

## THE NEW DROP

Hangings took place in public until an act of Parliament in 1868. After that, executions were taken indoors and carried out within the Castle walls. The New Drop in the castle continued with the executions, but behind closed doors.

## HUNG DRAWN & QUARTERED – MICKLEGATE BAR

There was no worse crime than to betray the crown. Thus, treason bestowed the worst punishment. If convicted, you were dragged through the streets, hung until not quite dead, and cut down alive. You would then be 'drawn', which involved pulling your guts out; a particular skill was to rip the heart out, so you could see it beating while you were still alive. The executioner would then throw the dissected organs into a fire in front of the convicted criminal.  Finally, the body was beheaded. Which, if the prisoner was still alive at this point, might have seemed like a relief.

Finally, executioners chopped the remain of the body into pieces, usually four, hence the quartering. Then the body parts were boiled in salted water and covered in pitch to preserve them. This severe form of punishment took place at York Castle or on the Knavesmire, and the four quarters of the convict's body placed on the four Bars of York, and the head on Micklegate Bar, but sometimes on the other Bars or Foss or Ouse Bridge if Micklegate Bar was full. (York Civic Trust) The heads would remain in place for years.

The last heads were William Connolly and James Mayne –placed on the Micklegate Bar after the Jacobite rebellion of 1746.

## DISSECTION

The government brought in the Murder Act of 1752. This Act included providing better control of the horrific crime of murder and instilling some further terror and peculiar mark of infamy to the punishment. The proposed intention to deter people from killing others. The government believed that the punishment should fit the crime. Thus, this stance denied the prisoner any prospect of a decent burial. On the contrary, their sentence would include the dread of knowing their body's final fate would be the public anatomisation and the dissection of their dead body. Furthermore, the convict faced the possibility of knowing that their corpse would be on public display, hung in chains, and left to rot.

## GIBBETING

Gibbeting fashioned the practice of barbarously locking criminals in human-shaped cages and hanging them up for display in public areas as a warning to others. For those sentenced to anatomisation, crowds trooped through inns and other convenient sites to see bodies cut and spread open. The last place for the corpses was at the much more secluded anatomy rooms for medical research, where surgeons and medical trainees would dissect the dead body to extremities. These harsh public punishments attracted humiliation and disgrace on the condemned. They also stopped the interment of the body and performance of the customary religious and cultural rituals,  denying both the condemned and their family the comfort and finality of a decent burial.

This Act also stipulated that a person found guilty of murder should have their sentence executed two days after being sentenced unless the third day was a Sunday, in which case the execution would take place the following Monday. No appeal system existed in those days. There was no such thing as being innocent or wrongly accused. All these barbaric practices continued for over 80 years until 1828, when they stopped.

The Anatomy Act of 1832 gave licence to doctors and teachers of anatomy and bona fide medical students to dissect donated bodies of executed murderers after their deaths, both male and female. This Act put a stop to the evil Act of grave robbing and the illicit trade in corpses. Fresh corpses were much in demand to improve medicine teaching and see how the body functioned.

## CAPITAL CRIMES

Crimes such as murder, cutting and maiming, piracies and mutinies, burglary, housebreaking, privately stealing in dwellings, highway robbery, horse and sheep-stealing, arson, and high treason extort money by threat, causing abortion. All received a death sentence if found guilty.

## TRANSPORTATION

With the American War of Independence outbreak in 1776. Colonial ports virtually ceased accepting convict ships. Subsequently, the British government needed a new colony to send convicted criminals. Under the Act of 1718, early transportees sailed to the American Colonies, such as Maryland or Virginia, often for very trivial crimes. Eventually, they chose Botany Bay. On 13th May 1787, the First Fleet, carrying 778 convicts, departed from Portsmouth. However, authorities soon discovered that the water supply was inadequate, the winds high, and the ground swampy and looked for an alternative location. Thus the coast of New South Wales, recently explored by Captain James Cook, became the penal colony for many of Yorkshire's convicted criminals.  With the worst convicts sent to Van Diemen's Land (Tasmania).

Transportation to New South Wales and Tasmania continued until 1850 and, after that, to Western Australia. The transport of convicts ceased entirely in 1868 when a system of penal servitude then superseded it.

Authorities expected prisoners under sentence of transportation to abide by the following rules. In ordinary cases, male convicts will be subjected to three periods of discipline before they serve out the term of their sentence or obtain a conditional pardon in the country of their transportation.

1. The first period is to be spent in separate confinement.
2. The second period will be passed at Hard Labour on public works under strict discipline for a period proportioned to the sentence.
3. The third period is to be passed with a ticket of leave in one of the Majesty's Colonies.

Sentence of life – reckoned at 24 years

Families of the convicts – arrangements and assistance given towards defraying the expense of the passage to the colony to the wives and families of well-conducted convicts, providing that private sources were providing the remainder of the costs.

Sentences were harsh and often for petty offences. For example, in 1826, at the General Quarter Sessions for the East Riding, sitting at Beverley, three men, John Beauchamp, John Levett and Richard Claybourne, faced criminal charges for stealing rags from the local paper mill. All three were found guilty and transported to Australia for seven years. Again, in Beverley, spinster Dawn Richardson was transported for seven years for stealing three screws from her workplace.

## SOME INTERESTING CASES FROM TYBURN & THE 'NEW DROP'

There were many executions over the years at both Tyburn and the 'New Drop' here are just a few interesting cases.

## DICK TURPIN 1739 – TYBURN

One of the most notable executions at Tyburn was John Palmer, known as the highwayman Dick Turpin. Turpin was hanged on Saturday the 7th

April 1739, having been found guilty of horse theft, and taken from the York Castle's condemned cell and driven in a horse-drawn cart through the imposing gateway of the castle and along Castlegate.

Crowds would line the route as prisoners made their way over Ouse Bridge, the only road bridge across the river. Then, along Ousegate and continuing up the steep slope of Micklegate, they would have driven through Micklegate Bar and onto Blossom Street, The Mount, and finally to the Tyburn, the site of the gallows. Turpin is buried at St George's graveyard, York.

Saturday, 30th April 1649, at the Lent Assizes, fourteen men and seven women were condemned to death in a very solemn manner by judge Thorpe. The latter informed them that fourteen of them would face execution for their rebellion. One woman Elizabeth Tomlinson was hanged and burned close to the gallows for the wilful murder of her bastard child. Twenty-nine-year-old Grace Bland also faced the hangman for blatantly setting fire to her mistress's house known by the sign of the Maypole in Clifton near York.

Emma Robinson, aged 25, known as Fair Emma, a native of Masham, hanged for poisoning her fellow servant Mary Wood through jealousy. Jane Lickise, aged 43, for the wilful murder of her maidservant Mary Lumley by strangling her whilst in her bed at Wetherby. She was hanged and burned. Fifty-three-year-old Hannah Meynell, described as a very stout woman, weighing at least 16 stone, was found guilty of wounding George Myers at Marston. After examination, her body donated to the surgeons of the city for dissection.

Isabella Billington, age 32 from Pocklington, faced execution for crucifying her mother on 5th January 1649. She also offered a calf and a cock for a burnt sacrifice. Her husband was also charged and hanged for being a participant in the crime.

## HONEST JOHN – THE PIPER

One of the strangest tales from Tyburn was that of piper John Bartendale, a young piper, who despite little evidence, was found guilty of theft and sentenced to hang on 27th March 1634. With the deed done, he remained for three-quarters of an hour on the gibbet. He was presumed dead, cut down and buried nearby. A short time later, a gentleman belonging to the Vavasours of Hazelwood was riding by when he thought he saw some earth moving. He ordered his men to look closely and was astounded to find that the buried man John Bartendale was still alive. Bewildered, John rubbed his eyes and asked, 'where am I?'.

Word soon got around York that an executed convict had survived. John was quickly re-arrested, taken back to York Castle and brought before the next Assizes. The presiding judge was amazed by the Act of providence bestowed upon this man that he granted the piper a full and free pardon.

After his release, John led an honest life, and he became a publican in the town. However, when asked about his experience of 'death', he encountered flashes of fire that darted around his eyes. He then blacked out.

To this day, York has a curious custom of raising a toast to honest John.

Hopefully, it does bring good luck.

# CHAPTER 1

## 1776. Flamborough Yorkshire. Elizabeth Boardingham & Thomas Aikney.

*Burning at the stake ©Public Domain.*

Flamborough on the Yorkshire coast, with its rugged coastline, a warren of natural coves, deep water cliffs, and accessible creeks, is the perfect location for smuggling. This area has many caves along the rocky shore, which provides the ideal place to hide illicit contraband. In the 18th and early 19th centuries, Tea, Brandy, Tobacco, Silk, and Cotton were the primary smuggled goods, but 'Geneva', an over-proofed Gin, was becoming a favourite of the households of Yorkshire.

Smuggling, on such a grand scale, required organisation, skill, and investment.

On the shore, the operation had three stages. First, the landing party, assisted by groups of locals, would lead the customs officers on a blind run, guiding them away from the actual intended landing places. The second stage involved moving the goods inland to the smugglers' houses, which had secret holes and cupboards, which were well-hidden from the prying eyes and the long arms of the customs officers. The final stage was to sell the products, and sometimes this would be as far away as Leeds, York or even London.

According to the press at the time, there were four smuggling vessels around Flamborough Head, constructed in such a way they could outrun several of his Majesty's cutters. So precise was their organisation it would only be by accident that one of them should get seized.

> *'T'is said these vessels carry about a thousand pound each week, sometimes three times that amount.' Onboard many may buy tea at three shillings, and as much 'Geneva' as you will, at thirteen pence a quart, it is this cheapness of this 'mother's ruin' that has increased the number of drunkards around our towns and villages.'* (Derby Mercury, 26th June 1767.)

John Boardingham, a Flamborough man, was one of the town's smugglers, not one of the organisers; he had neither the brains nor the money for that. Still, in the overall scheme of things, John had his uses as he was one of the men who would be on the shore ready to carry the illicit contraband away to one of the many hiding holes.

John married a young local girl called Elizabeth, and the couple had five children. The trouble with John was that he was well known to the authorities. His face was a common sight at the quarterly assizes, often caught in the Act of coming and going from the beach or on the cliffs armed with illegal goods. For his crimes, John perpetually spent time in York Castle for up to three months at a time. With such an unreliable husband, his wife grew tired of trying to make ends meet and provide food and shelter for her children whilst her husband served his time at her Majesty's pleasure. It was whilst he was doing yet another three-month prison sentence, she met Thomas Aikney.

Aikney was six years older than Elizabeth, a native of Thwing Upon the Wolds. He showed Elizabeth attention and affection  –  something that was long gone in her marriage to John. Elizabeth was smitten with Thomas, and when her husband was away for yet another stint in prison, she moved her lover into her house, an act that caused a stir in the close-knit Flamborough community.

On her husband's release from prison, she had finally had enough of her husband's criminal ways, and she left him and her children to set up home in Lincolnshire with Thomas, the love of her life. However, it was hardly love's young dream. Unfortunately, things didn't go to plan, as after three months in Lincoln, the landlord discovered that the couple were not married and threw them out. Elizabeth had no choice but to return to her home town where she asked forgiveness from her husband, who reluctantly took her back.

Thomas was still in love with Elizabeth, and not wanting to be too far away from her, he rented lodgings in Flamborough. Inevitably, the couple rekindled their relationship. Thomas wanted Elizabeth to elope with him, but that was impossible with her husband still on the scene. A neighbour heard Elizabeth say, 'If my husband were dead, Tom and I would be married, and I would no longer have to live like a whore and he a rogue, as we have had to live for some time now!'

Months after their return to Yorkshire, the couple carried on with their clandestine relationship whilst Elizabeth was still living with her husband and children.

On 14th February 1776, eight days after returning home to Flamborough around eleven o'clock, Elizabeth woke her husband up to tell him she had heard a noise at the door. Concerned, he quickly put on his trousers, shirt and waistcoat and went downstairs to the back door, having no suspicion of the terrible circumstance that would be waiting for him. Aikney lay in wait; upon seeing his lover's husband, Aikney rushed at him and plunged a knife straight into his thigh. He then stabbed him repeatedly on his left side, leaving the knife in the wound.

Elizabeth played her part well and ran outside shouting 'murder, murder'. In the meantime, Aikney escaped. A neighbour came to the dying man's assistance. The poor man was in a terrible state, and his situation was almost too shocking for words. Though just still alive, one of his hands was clutching the bloody knife embedded in his side, while his other hand was supporting his bowels which were falling out of his body. Incredibly, the victim remained in this same state till the following day, when he died in complete agony.

Thomas Aikney was found and arrested. The knife was a substantial piece of evidence, and the weapon was produced into court identified by the victim's and Elizabeth's nine-year-old daughter Mary and proved to belong to Aikney. When asked if he had anything to say, Aikney behaved penitently and acknowledged his guilt. He readily accepted the witness's testimony with composure and recognition and satisfaction that his lover Elizabeth Boardinghham was to share the same ignominious condemnation with him, as she was the primary cause of planning this terrible murder.

At the trial at York Assizes before Judge Sir Henry Gould, Elizabeth showed no emotion. Her calm attitude, boldness and general unconcern for the proceedings shocked the jury and all who saw her.  She insisted that she was not privy to the murder of her husband. The jury believed the opposite and saw straight through Elizabeth's cries of innocence and found both parties guilty.

The judge delivered his sentence. Despite Elizabeth not physically committing the murder and being second on the indictment for her part in the crime, she received a far harsher punishment. His Lordship said.

> *'Elizabeth Boardingham, your name stands second in the indict-
> ment. Yet as the law has distinguished the offence you have been
> found guilty with more particular disgrace than is ordinary, it is
> upon you that I shall first pass a sentence which from the nature
> of the offence deserves such a punishment. You have been found to
> abate your affections from your husband and transfer them away*

*from him to another man, who inspired you to commit much wickedness, and I feel it manifestly appears from the evidence provided that you ignited it into the breast of the other prisoner to commit the horrid crime of which you have been found guilty and that you wished for the murder of your husband which you The law of man consistent with that of the gospel has determined there is a submission due from a wife to her husband and subordination the husband has over his wife. Therefore this constitutes allegiance from the wife to the husband, and if this behaviour may transgress, then this is called by the small law treason. For this offence and to deter women from breaking their marriage vows. As we have heard throughout this trial with the evidence, we have heard. Were bound in duty both by the law of God and man, to have cherished and who ought to have had any comfort administered by you. The law has imposed a punishment of ignominy upon such offenders. You Elizabeth Boardingham shall be led from the Gaol from whence you came, and from Wednesday- day next you shall be drawn upon a hurdle to the place of execution, and there you will be burnt with fire until you are dead. Your body will be confined to the ashes.'* (Leeds Intelligencer, 16th April 1776.)

In today's times, it seems incredible that someone would receive such a severe sentence which, although an accomplice to murder and the instigator of the crime, should receive a harsher punishment than the actual murderer. However, in 1776 women were considered second class citizens to their husbands. Women were supposed to be loyal and serve their spouses unconditionally. Elizabeth had broken her vows in the public's eye, and her conviction was that of petty treason.

The judge said, 'Nevertheless, there is such a spirit of lenity in the common law of this country. Although this is the sentence you have received, and for my part, I could not believe that a sentence could in the strict letter of the law be more appropriate—Elizabeth Boardingham, you have justly been found guilty of a crime of the greatest magnitude. However, the law has allowed mitigation. First, you will be strangled at the stake. Then your body will be burnt with fire! In this instance, you have reason to admire the excellency of that constitution by which you have been tried and found guilty!'

The judge then addressed Thomas Aikney. 'As for you, Mr Aikney, you have only yourself to blame though you are in an unfortunate situation. I am persuaded and inclined to believe that this situation would not have happened if you had ignored the wishes of the female to which you became embroiled. This woman urged and pushed you to commit this horrific crime of murder. However, you must be sensible about how necessary it is to receive punishment for this terrible crime. From your behaviour so vicious and cruel towards the unfortunate deceased, so you can expect no mercy in this verdict. Both of you will reconcile yourselves to suffer the death penalty as described.'

It is difficult to see just what Elizabeth had to admire about such a generous concession within 'the spirit of lenity in the common law', a law that for over one hundred years thereafter condemned men, women, and children to capital punishment for the smallest of thefts. Nevertheless, she would be dead once the spectators witnessed her tied to a stake and her body burned to cinders.

Both prisoners were taken to York Castle to await execution, on 20th March 1776, at York Tyburn in front of a vast crowd of people. Some cheered and some booed as they watched the couple take their last journey, Thomas on a cart and Elizabeth on a sledge from York Castle to Tyburn. The trip took them over Ouse Bridge, up the steep slope of Micklegate and the Mount to where the hanging would occur. Reports say that as Elizabeth left her lover to receive her final fate, the couple shook hands and saluted each other. Elizabeth asked Thomas for a kiss, he refused.

Elizabeth Boardingham paid the ultimate price for betraying her husband and for not abiding by the natural hierarchy, which in this era ranked men above women. Therefore Elizabeth's crime was deemed not simply just murder but petty treason.

Public executions were well-attended affairs, and contemporary reports detail the cries of women on the pyre as they were burned alive. It later became commonplace as in Elizabeth's case for the executioner to strangle the convict, and the body burned post-mortem. Thomas Aikney's body was delivered to the surgeons at Leeds Infirmary for dissection.

Elizabeth Boardingham was the last female in Yorkshire to be burnt at the stake.

## BURNING AT THE STAKE

This severe legal punishment was used for both sexes in England and Wales to punish heresy, coining (counterfeiting), and matricide. As with Elizabeth Boardingham for petty and high treason, as men were considered superiors in law.

Males were hung, drawn, and quartered, but this was considered inappropriate for women as it would involve nudity.

Witches are often associated with burning at the stake. However, this horrific deed did not happen in England, only in Scotland, where both men and women could face this punishment if convicted.

The first burning in Britain was recorded in 1222 when a church deacon was found guilty of embracing the Jewish faith to marry a Jew. However, the law changed in 1790 when the government passed the Treason Act of 1790, and hanging substituted for coining offences. Catherine Hayes was the last female in England to be burned for petty treason in 1790. She died at Tyburn, London, for the murder of her husband.

# CHAPTER 2

## 1809. Leeds – Mary Bateman – The Yorkshire Witch.

*Damn her name to everlasting Fame.*

*Mary Bateman mixes the poison © Wikimedia Commons.*

If this were a tale of Fiction, it would be incredulous, but it is a true story of one of the worst criminal people to have ever lived. Mary Bateman had no scruples. She didn't care who she duped or robbed and never gave it a second thought that her devilish, ruthless actions would  cause her unsuspecting victims unmeasurable distress. She was a wicked witch in every sense of the word.

Born Mary Harker in 1768, she was the daughter of Benjamin and Ann Harker, small farmers from Aisenby in Topcliffe, Thirsk, in the North Riding. Whilst her exact date of birth is unknown, we do know that she received baptism in the local church of St Columba's. Her parents ensured that Mary received a good education. She was a quick learner and soon learned how to read and write. However, from childhood, Mary was artful, devious, and her morals were lacking. Her career as a petty thief started from an early age and became habitual, her thefts maturing as she grew. Mary's neighbours were sick and tired of her wayward ways and complained to her parents, but instead of chastising their daughter, her parents either laughed at her waywardness or pardoned her.  Thirsk Magistrates Court admonished Mary's father for allowing his daughter to become a 'cunning child, skilled in small thefts'. One time Mary stole a pair of leather Moroccan and hid them in her father's barn. Mary proclaimed her innocence when someone found the shoes, saying she had seen them on the road.

As she grew older, Mary's pilfering ways became bolder and more frequent. She spent her time around gipsies and acquired from them their skill of fortune-telling and potion-making. Thieving had quickly turned into a habit for the young girl. Her father's concern for his daughter worsened, and he found it impossible to get her to obey him, so he took matters into his own hands and, hoping it would improve her, her father sent her away into domestic service.

Mr Harker's plan for his unruly daughter backfired, and Mary had at least five service jobs in six years. Two of her former employees suffered 'strange pains and agonies and were near death' whilst Mary was employed. In 1787 Mary hurriedly left Thirsk in very suspicious circumstances and moved to York, not even waiting to collect her clothing or wages. She wasn't in York long as she left a year later once again under the suspicion of robbing her mistress.

Mary's next port of call was Leeds, where she worked as a mantua maker (women's clothing), a profession she learned from her mistress during her residence in York. This profession suited her, as the servant girls would introduce her to their mistresses. It was around this time that she learned from her gipsy friends that she started fortune-telling.

Mary, the sorcerer, was well on her way. Leeds suited Mary, and she lived and worked in the same area for four years when on 26th February 1792, at St Peter's Church after courting for only three weeks, she married John Bateman, an honest, hardworking wheelwright besotted with his young bride. It does seem that John Bateman was naive or turned a blind eye to his wife's misdemeanours.

Leeds in the 18$^{th}$ century was an upcoming industrial town with new warehouses constructed throughout the city. Work was scarce. Unemployment high, with people fighting for limited jobs. Wages were poor, with men earning an average wage of twelve shillings and women and children two or three shillings. Most working people lived in small cottages, often in yards or courts behind the town's main streets. They had few possessions except for basic furniture and cooking utensils. People had to manage their money carefully, ensuring they had enough for rent, food and other basics like candles, fuel, clothes, and linen. There would be no money left for doctors or medicines. The opening of Leeds General Infirmary (1767) was welcomed with open arms from both the rich and the poor as it provided medical assistance to all for free.

The newly married Mr and Mrs Bateman took a small house in the yard of Mr Wells spirit merchant in Briggate. The house was decorated well and way beyond the couple's financial means and presumably furnished from the profits of one of Mary's crimes. Her husband appears to have ignored or trusted his wife completely. John turning a blind eye didn't stop Mary from conning him too. One day she went to her husband's workshop in great distress, brandishing a letter telling him that Bateman's father, who was the town-crier for Thirsk, was dying. Concerned, John Bateman borrowed money from his employer for the journey. As he entered Thirsk, he was relieved to hear his father's voice in the street announcing a public auction. When John returned home to Leeds, excited to tell Mary that the letter was a hoax and thrilled that his father was alive and well. He found that Mary had ransacked the house and stripped it bare of all furniture and sold the lot; most probably, getting him out of the way was a decoy to compensate for another robbery she was involved in. On another occasion, her husband went to stay with friends, and when he returned, he found his wife had sold all his clothes.

Astonishingly, the couple stayed together and moved to Ebenezer Street, Leeds, where they managed to refurbish the house and take in lodgers.

On 17th January 1794, their first child Mary was born. However, motherhood didn't kerb Mary's criminal ways. One of her lodgers, Mr Dixon, complained that some of his possessions and money was missing from his box. Once again, Mary's thieving ways had caught up with her. Mr Dixon agreed not to press charges, but he demanded compensation for his losses.

Not long after her marriage, Mary returned to her art of fortune-telling and set up a 'cave of mystery' in Marsh Lane near Timble Bridge, Leeds, where she would proclaim to predict the future, to rid the unfortunate of evil spells. However, none of this she did in her name but under Mrs Moore's representation, who she said had supernatural powers because she was the 7th child of a 7th child. She soon developed a good reputation as a card reader and a seller of good luck charms.

Mary described as a neat person with good dress sense, a soft, caring, innocent, and open countenance. To the superstitions of the local people, Mary soon became an object of awe, her professing of dealing with the unseen taken as gospel truth. Butchers in Leeds meat market would not open their doors on a Monday until 'cunning Mary' had been duly fed by them, as she claimed a peculiar prayer over all sellers of 'dead flesh'.

In 1792, Joanna Southcott, a self-proclaimed prophet guided by the 'spirit of truth', said the Lord had visited her in great power to 'warn her of what was coming upon the whole earth.' In this year. In her spare time, she began writing by the dictates of the spirit. Joanna placed all her writings in a box (The Great Box) which, she proclaimed if opened, would change the world's future. Mary soon became a follower and a regular attendee of the newly formed 'cult' meetings.

Never one to be upstaged, Mary invented a similar incredible story of 'The Prophet Hen of Leeds'. Mary Bateman at that time was living at Black Dog Yard near the Bank, declaring that her hens could predict the future and forecast the end of the world! She charged one penny for visitors to witness this miracle, with some of the eggs having messages written on them saying 'Christ is Coming'. This message caused mass panic in the Leeds area, and devoutly religious people came from far and wide to witness this prophecy. But, of course, it was a scam. Mary had written these statements on the eggs herself and forced the eggs back inside the chicken to make it look like the chicken had laid these miraculous eggs naturally. The trouble was that as soon as the hen moved from the hen-nest, the poor bewildered creature produced egg normally. Nobody liked to insinuate to Mary that it was a fraud – just in case she put a spell on them.

Not owning their own house, the couple rented or took lodgings around Leeds. At High Court Lane, a fellow lodger discovered a silver watch, silver spoons, and two guineas belonging to him missing. The lodger threatened Mary. She proclaimed her innocence, but to keep him quiet, Mary returned his money. On another occasion, she duped a linen draper in Leeds, asking them to send three silk petticoats for a Miss Stephenson. She returned two but kept the other one. Miss Stephenson failed to pay for the other as Miss Stephenson didn't exist. Finally, The shopkeeper saw through Mary's charade but mistakenly took her for a poor milliner and forgave her.

A gentleman living in Meadow Lane, Leeds, bought a leg of mutton at the Shambles and directed the butcher to deliver the meat to his house. Mary was always on the watch for her prey, and she went to the bridge the butcher's boy would have to cross. On seeing him, she pretended to be the gentleman's servant, and she chastised the boy for taking his time in delivering the meat. Mary slapped the young boy on the back with fake exasperation, telling him she would take it to her master herself. Finding out that the meat had been handed over to a servant on the bridge over an hour ago infuriated the man. He complained to the butcher. When he heard the 'servants' description, the gentleman recognised Mary Bateman, who he had seen lurking in the same butcher's shop that morning. He went to where she was living at the Old Assembly Rooms, Kirkgate, where the first thing he saw was his mutton roasting on the fire. Mary pleaded poverty and admitted her theft, and offered to pay for the meat. The gentleman accepted, and the matter was closed.

In January 1796, her second child John was born, but motherhood didn't curtail her wickedness. In this same year, a tremendous fire broke out at a manufacturer in Leeds. The heat intensity brought walls crashing down and many people, including children, lost their lives. Having no scruples, Mary saw an opportunity to cash in on other people's misery, and she went to see Miss Maud, a local lady well known for her kindness and generosity. In tears and full of false compassion, Mary explained to the charitable lady that she knew a lady, a victim of the fire who had lost a child who had no money for bedding to lay the dead child out and begged her to lend her a pair of sheets. This request was complied with,

Mary pleaded this same case three times, the outcome the same. Her devious abysmal crimes did not end here. She manipulated the suffering of the actual victims of this horrendous accident and went round Leeds proclaiming to be a nurse at the General Infirmary. She collected all the old linen she could beg, 'to dress the wounds of the injured, she said, but she pawned it all for her benefit, but instead of the alleged intended purpose, the bedding went straight to the pawnshop.

John Bateman, disgusted and embarrassed by his wife's vile ways, joined the Supplementary Militia. Unfortunately for him, he took Mary with him. Maybe he thought a change of scenery might change her. It didn't. It made her worse; she practised her old tricks and learned new ones. The couple returned to Leeds taking up residence in Marsh Lane, near Timble Bridge and soon gained a very uncanny reputation. Still, she was in great demand amongst the unassuming country people of Leeds as a witch – to use the words of one person she duped, 'Bateman knew and could do by the aid of others.'

Mary's first experiment in witchcraft began when she tried to convince her neighbour, Mrs Greenwood, that her husband was in great peril and soon to be accused of committing a serious crime. Nothing could save him unless four pieces of gold, four pieces of leather, four pieces of blotting paper, and four brass screws were given to Mary to Mrs Moore to 'screw down' the guards. If she failed to do this, then her husband would be dead by the morning. Mrs Greenwood had no gold and did not intend to beg or steal it, so her husband would have to take his chances. Mrs Greenwood had the common sense to emancipate herself from Mary's cunning evil spells.

The family of Barzillai Stead were not so lucky and became Mary's next victim. Knowing that the poor man had failed in business, Mary preyed on his misery and conjured her wicked artful spell of deception to convince the worried man that the bailiffs were in continual pursuit of him. The best thing he could do was to enlist in the forces and share his sign-up bounty with her and the imaginary wise woman Mrs Moore. Her next deception was to arouse the jealousy of his wife. Mary confided in her that when her husband went into the regiment, he intended to take a young girl from Vicar Lane, Leeds, who she told his wife was pregnant by him. To prevent this, it would be necessary to 'screw down' (stop) this rival woman, and the wife must give Mary three half-crowns and Mary had to put the coal at the woman's door in Vicar Lane, then place it on the fire. Two pieces of coal. The coal was to blacken the clothes of this imaginary woman, so she could not 'run' off with the woman's husband if she had no clothes to wear.

Knowing nothing of this, Stead set off to join his regiment, leaving his vulnerable wife behind him and into the evil hands of this vile Leeds sorcerer. Wasting no time, Mary persuaded the woman it was necessary to pawn every value item in her house. The poor woman was pregnant and penniless with not a scrap of furniture. The Leeds Benevolent Society found her in a destitute situation and granted the woman a guinea, paid in monthly instalments. Heartlessly, Mary took eighteen shillings of this much-needed money.

On another occasion, she persuaded the woman that her husband's father intended to murder her, and only the powers of Mrs Moore could save her, but she needed money to stop this. Mary added that it was vital for her to find this money or the woman's eight-year-old daughter would become pregnant at age fourteen with an illegitimate child and that she would murder the child herself, or the seducer would murder her and the child. The only way to prevent this was to give Mary seventeen shillings for her to hand over to Mrs Moore, who would give the child a silver charm to wear around her arm until the danger had passed, which would then be cut from the child's arm three months later once the bubble burst. Once more, the woman scraped together the money by selling all she had left. Nothing else remained, except for a few tools left by her husband before he signed up. Unrelenting, Mary insisted these also be sold. Finally, Mrs Stead couldn't take much more and almost driven to madness and, through stress and anxiety, thought her only escape was to kill herself. Desperate, the poor woman threw herself into the River Calder. Fortunately, someone saw her and saved her. With help from her neighbours, she began to realise the frauds and impositions of Mary Bateman and that she had got herself tied up in her wicked web.

Now enlightened, Mrs Stead freed herself from the evil woman's grasp. At first, she found it difficult to believe that Mary had conned her. She thought it impossible. Enraged, she confronted Bateman and threatened her that she would have committed to prison for fraud if she did not give her the money to redeem her pledged possessions. Mary soon gave the woman her four guineas back and returned all her furniture and possessions.

Another of the Bateman's neighbours, a poor man who tried his best to provide for his family with a horse and cart, fell ill and died, leaving a widow and four children. The wife is the children's stepmother. Never one to miss an opportunity, Mary friended this wife and persuaded her that the eldest son who was fifteen intended to sell all the property his father had left and keep all the money for himself. Mary persuaded her that the only thing she could do was to sell the horse and cart and furniture and leave Yorkshire. Infuriated, the widow took Mary's advice and left the children and a share of the proceeds with Mary. Mary pocketed the cash and sent the orphaned children to the workhouse. What happened to the stepmother is not known as she was never seen or heard of again.

The Bateman's third child Marie was born on 25th October 1801. Once more, motherhood did not get in her way. Always astute, Mary considered the knockback she had with Mrs Greenwood. To avoid another setback, she invented another character, Miss Blythe from Scarborough, who Mary described as the 'the wisest woman, the greatest witch and the best spell-seller in all Yorkshire.' The rural people of Yorkshire believed Mary's story and came from all over the area for her help.

Now living at St Peter's Square, Quarry Hill, Leeds, she met two maiden Quaker sisters named Kitchen, who owned a draper-linen shop near St Peter's Square. Mary friended the women and became their confidant. She helped them out in the shop, at their home, deluding the sisters that she knew Mrs Moore and Miss Blythe who could predict their futures. The unsuspecting sisters soon came under Mary's grips. In early September 1803, one of the sisters became sick with a mysterious and painful illness. On Mary's instructions, a doctor was not allowed to attend to the desperately ill woman. Instead, Mary was the one who procured the sick woman's medicines.

Within a week, the lady was dead. An eminent doctor who attended the sister was suspicious. He became convinced that poison was involved, so much so that he had every cooking vessel in the house examined. He even suggested that the poison attributed to the killing of flies around the house. He wanted to do a post-mortem on the dead sister's body. Unfortunately, this was not allowed, and soon after, there was no one left to give permission. The mother of the dead woman who had recently departed from Wakefield to Leeds in good health to nurse her remaining daughter was just in time to see her youngest child die. A close family friend called at the house. She seemed to be suppressing a secret that she wished to discuss. However, strangely enough, the woman herself died before she had the chance to say what was on her mind.

A mere ten days had elapsed since the first sister's death and that of the mother—the cause of the three deaths attributed to cholera. However, Mary had to act quickly. She had to stop the neighbours from entering the Kitchen's house. She told everyone that both sisters and the mother had died from the Plague. Surprisingly, nobody questioned her story, and the house shunned. As she predicted, no one wanted to be in the same place as a terrible deadly contagious disease. The house was locked up with a 'do not enter' warning sign on the door. Only Mary had a key.

Sometime after the deaths, creditors looked upon the lady's possessions and were astounded to find nothing left. All the contents, both household and personal, were gone. Even the books belonging to the shop accounts that the careful, frugal businesswomen were most particular about completing were missing. Perhaps the reason for this was that these books contained confirmation of Mary's unpaid haberdashery items. The creditors had to settle for their outstanding invoices paid at the derisory sum of 8d in the pound.

Mary had her fourth child George on 19th April 1804, but sadness followed the family when three-year-old Mary died of fits and buried in St Peter's Church, Leeds. Life cannot have been easy for the Bateman children with their mother's reputation and regularly moving to a new house. Fortunately for them, they were a little too young to realise the full implications of their mother's actions.

Two young servant girls working in Leeds had for a long time been under Mary's spells. Mary had persuaded them to rob their mother of her possessions and steal the family Bible. Knowing that insinuations were beginning to stir, Mary sent the girls away to Manchester with strict instructions not to speak to each other. If they disobeyed this order, then the charms would not work. The poor girls were almost destitute and hopeless. By chance, they bumped into each other on the streets of Manchester and both burst into tears. Comparing notes, they realised they were both the victims of a sophisticated con artist. They wrote to friends in Leeds who confronted Mary and demanded the girl's property back. Reluctantly, she agreed.

William Perigo, a cloth manufacturer from Bramley, married his wife Rebecca (nee Stockdale) twenty years ago. Rebecca was the daughter of Joshua Stockdale, a stonemason from Bramley. In twenty years of marriage, Rebecca had not suffered a day's illness, and her health was generally robust, but recently she had terrible chest pains, and William thought his wife had a curse upon her. A doctor had attended the sick woman and declared nothing further he could do to help her because Rebecca had been 'evil washed' and the case was beyond his skill. Rebecca's niece, a servant girl, named Sarah Stead, recommended that she make an early appointment with Mary Bateman. Mary soon took up the challenge and visited the Perigos at their house.

Hesitant, Mary said that she could not undertake the cure herself, but she knew a friend, a Miss Blythe who lived in Scarborough and all 'witches' paid tribute as 'Queen' who could help his sick wife. She said Miss Blythe could read the stars and collect from them the knowledge to remove all bodily and mental maladies. As a preliminary step, she required that the couple sends to her Rebecca Perigo's flannel petticoat so as Miss Blythe could collect from that article of dress a knowledge of her disorder and collect information from the planets. Mary told the couple that Miss Blythe would give them an answer in one week.

Obligingly, the Perigos sent the petticoat via Mary Bateman as directed. Soon after, they received a good answer. Miss Blythe said that before she could cure this extremely sick lady, she required four guinea notes presented to her via Mary Bateman only. These notes must be enclosed in a small bag and sewn into each of the four corners of the Perigo's bed on which the sick woman slept, and that these bags were to remain in place, untouched for eighteen months. Miss Blythe also told the worried couple that they must give a further four guineas to Mary Bateman or the charm would not work. The letter also directed Mr Perigo to obey the ritual and say specific prayers at Eventide and that they must not utter a word about this to anyone or the charm would break. Over several months Mary duped the couple into giving her many gifts and sums of cash. On one occasion, Mary met the Perigos on Kirkstall Bridge, where she accompanied the couple to their house, where no doubt Mary took a complete inventory of all their furniture. Mary, keeping up the pretence, gave the couple four guineas she alleged came from Miss Blythe in exchange for the same clean, fresh notes. The old letters Mary told them must once again be sewn into the four corners of the bed.

Two weeks later. Mary's son called at the Perigo's house with an unsealed letter, which he said his mother said was from Miss Blythe. In exchange, he needed two small pieces of iron made into the shape of a horseshoe from the ironmongers in Bramley, where the couple lived. When created, this horseshoe had to be nailed to the Perigo's front door by Mary, although not with a hammer, but with pincers, which Mary must send to Miss Blythe. William Perigo duly obliged and did as requested and sent the pincers to Leeds, where they were to remain for eighteen months.

Three weeks passed, the Perigos received another letter through the post from Miss Blythe, which said.

*'My Dear Friend.*
*You must go down to Mary Bateman's house at Leeds on Tues-*
*day next and carry two guinea notes and give them to her, and*
*she will exchange them for the same which I have sent her from*
*Scarbor- ough, you must buy me a small cheese with this money*
*about 6-8 lb in weight and take it to Mary Bateman's house. Mary*
*will send it to me via coach. You must burn this letter once you*
*have read it.*

A week later, another letter was received, again from Miss Blythe requesting the same amount of money. The Perigos received similar requests every two weeks. Finally, Mary became bolder with her wishes and asked the couple for various furniture, clothes, and other property. Overall, the Perigos paid 'Miss Blythe' a total of £70, quite a considerable amount of money in 1806. Besides this, the couple had given Mary the following.

*1 Goose, A Goose eye, Tea Caddy, Several sheets, A counterpane,*
*a piece of woollen cloth, a silk handkerchief, a silk shawl, a light*
*coloured skirt, a cotton gown, two pillowcases, a waistcoat, 60lb*
*of butter, seven pieces of meat, tea & sugar 200 eggs, a pair of*
*stockings, a pair of shoes, silk stockings, 3 yards of linen cloth, ten*
*stones of malt, a piece of beef, three bottles of spirits, two table*
*cloths, two wooden barrels, and two napkins.*

By now, Mary must have realised that she was stretching this extortion of these two desperate people to the limit. Not one to give in easily, she sent a package of honey to the Perigos with instructions for them to bring it to Mary's house where unique ingredients would be added to it which had been prepared by Miss Blythe herself. Mary also instructed the couple to add a separate powder to the mixture each day. The Perigos must eat puddings starting on 11th May with this unique honey for six consecutive days. Any break in this arrangement would mean that the charms would not work. The only stipulation was that under no circumstances were they to let their child eat any, and once more, it was vital to burn this letter after reading it.

William Perigo, desperate to see his wife's health restored, did as was asked of him and watched as Mary added a white powder to the honey. The letter also stated that on 25th May, Miss Blythe would visit Mrs Perigo, and she must declare, 'God bless you that I ever found you out.' The Perigos obeyed Mary, and for the first five days, they found they had no flavour. However, on the sixth day, Mr Perigo couldn't manage more than one mouthful before becoming overwhelmingly nauseous; his wife managed to take a spoonful of the honey as instructed, so desperate was she not to break the charm. Mr Perigo slowly recovered, but Mrs Perigo continued to take more of the sickly mixture. William lay beside his emaciated wife, whose mouth had by now turned black, and she could not open it without help. She pleaded with her husband that she could not die happy unless he promised her he would wait until Miss Blythe suggested before he opened the bags and retrieved their possessions. It was this promise that stopped William from coming forward sooner. At the end of the week, the couple was found in a terrible state by a neighbour. On Sunday, 17th May 1807, Rebecca died. On examination of her body, doctors took no further action to ascertain the cause of her death, even though a surgeon expressed the belief that she had taken poison.

Two days later, a letter arrived from Miss Blythe. The content read that Rebecca had died because she tried to open the bags. Furthermore, she gave strict instructions to William that if he tried to touch the enchanted bags, Rebecca would rise from the grave and touch his face with death's cold hand, rendering him paralysed on one side. Fear had long since plagued the grief-stricken Mr Perigo, yet he still believed in Mary's charms. After the death of his wife, he continued to see Mary, who professed that she thought that Rebecca could not have followed the instructions given by Miss Blythe correctly and she must have overeaten the honey.

The Bateman family still lived in Leeds but moved to a new house at Campfield, Water Lane, where one of the neighbours named Snowdon became a new profitable subject for the artful woman. The wife worried that one of her children would drown. Most likely, an idea planted in her head by the resourceful sorceress. To save this poor child from a watery grave, Mary naturally offered her services through the ever-eventful Miss Blythe, who Mary said lived in Thirsk. Soon after, Mary received a letter from the eminent elusive lady, who in her wisdom suggested that the Snowdon family sew the family silver into the couple's bedding and they should give Mary Bateman 12 guineas which the trusted Mary would exchange them for the same. More letters followed. Urgent concern was for the daughter who would become a prostitute unless they took immediate preventative action. Mary claimed that the family must leave Leeds and move to Bowling, Bradford, for the charms to work. The family were allowed to take their bed with them containing the charms. Miss Blythe insisted that all the furniture and all belongings were to remain in the house and the key lodged in the safe and capable hands of Mary Bateman. The Snowden's were desperate to open the corners of the bed and bring out the family silver, but Mary insisted that this would have severe consequences for the whole family. They could open the bags when the time was right, but Mary urged the family to take a draft made by Miss Blythe and administered by Mary before this. Fortunately, for the Snowden's, they did not take the deadly powder.

As agreed, the family moved to Bradford. One evening, Mr Snowden enjoyed a drink in the local tavern when he caught the headline 'Witchcraft, Murder, Credulity' from The Leeds Mercury, dated 22nd October 1809. Mary Bateman had faced trial for the frauds committed on William Perigo and the wilful murder of his wife Rebecca, who had died two years earlier. This sensation spread quickly through the Yorkshire towns and villages, and Mr Snowden could not believe what he read. Enraged, he rushed home to his wife and together, they ripped open the folds of the bed, where instead of silverware, there were lumps of coal.

Mr Snowden hurried to his house in Leeds, which he thought he had left in the safe hands of Mary Bateman. However, when opening the door, he found the silence of an empty room. There was none of his furniture and no possessions. The penny dropped. Mr Snowden realised he had been duped and went immediately to the Batemans house to recover his property.

The police arrested John Bateman for fraud as either an accomplice or a perpetrator. He came up for trial at the next assizes. Lucky for him, the jury acquitted him despite evidence coming to light that it was he who moved the Perigo's bedstead from the public house in Leeds, where Mr Perigo had left it for transportation to Miss Blythe. John took it to his workplace then later took it home, saying that he had bought it. John's character (compared to his wife) was good, having worked for the same employer as a wheelwright for sixteen years without a day off. Indeed, he must have wondered where all these household goods and possessions were coming from and cannot have been entirely ignorant of his wife's misdemeanours.

Eighteen months had now passed since the charms were sewn into the Perigo's bed, now deep in debt, and with his creditors becoming impatient, William was comforted by the belief that his wealth was still intact and safely sewn into bags attached to his bed. On 19th October 1808, driven by bravery, he and his friend John Rogerson opened the bags and was shocked and dismayed to find they contained nothing but old coins, bits of tin and a few button tops, dried cabbage leaves and a few farthings. Reality finally dawned on the gullible and all too trusting William Perigo. Realising he had been tricked and had been too trusting, and now he was a widow, a pauper, and he was without property and with his constitution ruined. He rushed to Mary Bateman's house, who unashamedly told him, 'Aye, that's what you get for being in too great a hurry. You've opened them too soon!' 'Too soon! I don't think so,' replied the angry man. 'Too late, more like!' Outraged, Perigo told Mary that he would bring three or four men down to see her the following day. Mary resisted, 'don't do that,' she cried, 'that would cause hully balloo.' The couple agreed to meet the following day outside the Navigation Bank Leeds centre. Unknown to Mary at this meeting, two men were watching her from across the street. As soon as this dawned on her, she feigned sickness and began to wretch.

Early morning on 21st October 1808, the Chief Constable of Leeds arrested Mary Bateman for fraud and the wilful murder of Rebecca Perigo.

The police took Mary to York Castle to stand trial. When brought up before the magistrates, she admitted in part that Miss Blythe did not exist and that she had made it all up. At last, the artful sorceress's evil ways ended. The police searched the house for over five hours, some of Mr Perigo's possessions were recovered and taken as evidence.

## THE TRIAL

The trial of Mary Bateman for the wilful murder of Rebecca Perigo started on 17th March 1809 at York Castle. Sir Simon Le Blanc 1748-1816 was the presiding judge with a jury of eleven men. Evidence of the handwriting of the alleged Miss Blythe was compared with the writing of Mary Bateman and found to be an identical match. Police constables searched the Scarborough area, but not surprisingly, Miss Blythe did not exist.

Throughout the trial, Mary pleaded her innocence. Yes, she had taken some money, but she knew nothing about giving anyone any pills, powders, or honey, and she had not poisoned Rebecca Perigo. Unfortunately, the evidence against her proved otherwise.

Sir Simon Le Blanc summed up and told the jury that to bring in a guilty verdict. The jury had to be satisfied on three points. These points were. One, Rebecca died from poisoning. Two that the poison had been administered, with the knowledge and contrivance of Mary Bateman. Three, that Mary intended to poison and ultimately kill Rebecca Perigo. He reminded them that although there was a strong case against Mary for systematically defrauding the Perigos, this did not make her automatically guilty of murder.

After consulting for just twelve hours, the jury returned a verdict. The evidence of criminality and murder was overwhelming. Following the usual procedure, His Lordship asked Mary if she had anything to say about why death should not be pronounced on her.

Dramatically, breaking into floods of tears, she pleaded her belly. In other words, she claimed to be twenty-three weeks pregnant. The law at the time stated that if a prisoner was four and a half months pregnant, an old statute where the underlying protection was to the unborn child, and that validity was not viable until there was a 'quickening' of the unborn foetus. Therefore, until the baby is born, there can be no prosecution. Knowing Mary's character was sceptical, the judge ordered twelve matrons to examine her to establish the truth. A sense of terror fled As a result, the judge ordered the court doors to be locked. The females in the courtroom made a rush for the exits as nobody wanted anything to do with this horrid evil woman. They certainly didn't want to touch her intimately. Eventually, an empanelled jury of matrons examined her. They found her not to be pregnant, so he ordered her to be hanged by the neck until she was dead. She was forty-one years of age and had her infant child John with her in prison until the time came to fulfil her sentence.

Mary maintained an air of mystery whilst in prison, although the Leeds Intelligencer reported that she continued to take money from other prisoners reading their horoscopes whilst she was there. On the day before the execution, she wrote to her husband enclosing her wedding ring, which she insisted must go to her daughter. To the very end, Mary proclaimed her innocence. Yes, she knew she had robbed people, but murder!, she was not guilty of murder. 'I have made my peace with God, and I am easy in mind. Tomorrow will end-all here, and the Lord will come for me after that.'

On 20th March 1809, at eleven o'clock in the morning, the streets of York were packed. Castlegate was impassable, with every Inn and boarding house in the town fully booked. People travelled from all over the country to witness the demise of the Yorkshire Witch. Perhaps some people imagined that Mary being the artful dodger she was, would rise from the scaffold and fly off on her broomstick. But, unfortunately, Mary wasn't alone on the podium. There was also a soldier from York who also executed for murder.

The executioner was William 'Mutton' Curry from Thirsk, nicknamed as he had been convicted twice for sheep stealing. While waiting for transportation to Australia, the post of hangman came up, and he accepted it. Thus his conveyance to the colonies reprieved.

The hour of the execution drew near, and the executioner asked Mary if she had any final words. 'Yes, I'm innocent.' After that, the crowd was deathly silent, the hangman did his job, and Mary was gone.

The woman who had caused such misery and suffering to so many people was dead. Her dead body was cut down and taken by cart to the surgeon's room at Leeds General Infirmary for dissection, which was allowed for medical training under the Murder Act of 1752. Unbelievably, her remains were put on view to the public at a charge of three-pence per person. Incredibly and somewhat morbidly, over two thousand people viewed Furthermore, pieces of her skin were tanned and sold and, on some occasions, made into objects such as cups. Finally, between the years of 1997-2015, the skeleton of the Yorkshire Witch was placed morbidly on public display at the Thackray Museum in Leeds. It is now in storage at the anatomy department at Leeds Medical school.

* * *

John Bateman most certainly did not live a charmed life after the death of his wife. Where the proceeds of Mary's years of crime went is not known, but it wasn't on her family. Guilty by association, John found himself in extreme poverty. He had to sell all his furniture, he had numerous unpaid debts, and his reputation was in tatters. Sadly, baby John who Mary had suckled to the last day before her execution, died aged three.

* * *

R.I.P to the many victims of Mary Bateman, especially Rebecca Perigo and the Kitchen family.

# CHAPTER 3

## 1857. Exley Head, Keighley –
## The Keighley Workhouse Poisoning –
## John & Barbara Sagar.

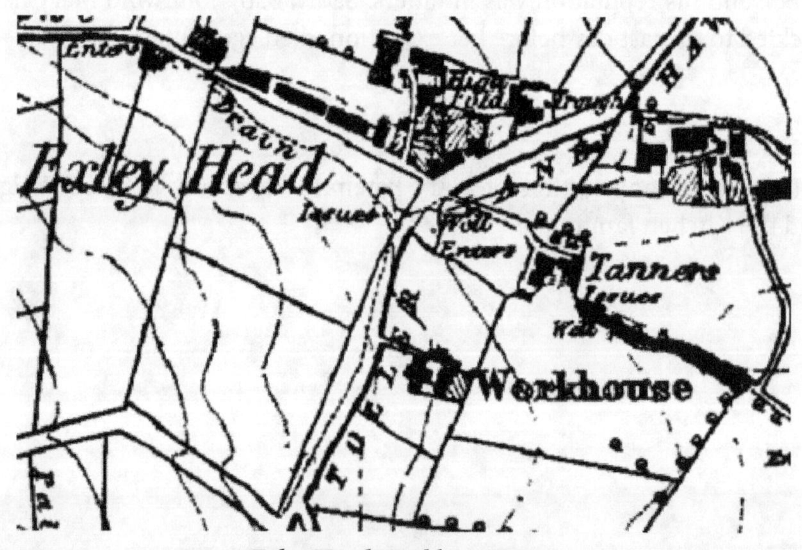

*Exley Head Workhouse 1852.*

Childhood sweethearts twenty-year-old Barbara Scarborough and twenty-six-year-old John Sagar married on Wednesday 29th August 1838 at the Superintendent's Registrar office in Keighley. The couple had been neighbours from the rural village of Cullingworth just a couple of miles from Haworth, where the Bronte family resided.

It seems Barbara and John had plenty of sadness in their lives as Barbara gave birth to nine children, who all sadly died before the age of four. All nine children are buried in Haworth churchyard not too far from Bronte Parsonage.

John Sagar had a variety of jobs. He spent twelve years as a painter, which he gave up to become a druggist. He subsequently left this business to become a publican in Cullingworth, where he and his wife were landlord and landlady for only two years.

In April 1852, the Sagar's accepted a job as Master and Matron of The Exley Head Workhouse, a crumbling flea-infested farmhouse owned by a farming family called Tonson. The initial intended use for this property was education, yet in 1739 it became the local workhouse. A parliamentary report written in 1777 stated that it had forty inmates. This filthy crumbling workhouse was condemned in 1844 and labelled 'a mere third-rate farmhouse', which, despite these damming recommendations, would not be replaced until 1860. This same government inspector said this workhouse was so dirty that vermin dropped from the ceiling like flies and that staff were encouraged to wear light coloured clothes as it was easier to spot fleas and pick them off. So, why the Sagar's would want to leave their respectable affluent home in Cullingworth where John had established himself as a painter and move lock stock and barrel into such disease-ridden and filthy surroundings is a mystery. Reports also suggest that following an inspection by the poor law commissioners in 1847, the workhouse's management was grossly mismanaged, and the workhouse was far too small for the accommodation required.

Workhouses came about because of an act passed in 1601 called 'The Act for the relief of the Poor.' This act required parishes to be legally responsible for the poor living within their boundaries and payment to provide for these unfortunate people collected from land and property owners. This scheme came with much opposition. People disagreed that the wealthy should feed the poor and give them money. Landowners were up in arms and branded the poor lazy and immoral who refused to do an honest day's work, who bred enormous families while expecting to feed them on handouts. In 1723, in response to this, the government introduced the 'Workhouse Act', which offered food and basic shelter in exchange for hard work. The government did not intend the workhouses to be pleasant. Many people feared them, and to go into one was the last resort and considered shameful and degrading.

Yet, in August 1851, the Sagar's changed the course of their lives and instructed Auctioneer William Dean to advertise the entire contents of their house for sale. Surprisingly, and inexplicably with no reserve –not a recommended move, and at the time, this was most unusual. Does this unprecedented move give the impression that the couple needed a new start, or did the Sagar's need the money? However, the couple did seem to have some valuable property, and the sale included, amongst other things, quality flock beds, china, an American clock, a silver watch, teaspoons, five oil paintings and a stomach pump.

The position of Master of the Workhouse was important yet an insecure occupation. There was no pension and no regular holidays. The Master was held responsible for every drop and crumb consumed in the workhouse. The authorities regularly audited the records and paperwork, which was the responsibility of the master.

The authorities preferred a couple without dependent children so as not to be distracted from household family responsibilities, as the Sagar's children were all dead (a subject that caused much curiosity through the town of Cullingworth). The couple matched the requirements perfectly. The Workhouse Master, in his position, had considerable power and great control and influence over the other staff and the inmates. Scandals were inevitable, and abuse of power happened often.

John Sagar was ideally suited to his position, although he only had one arm (no records exist as to what happened to his missing arm), he ran the workhouse with a rod of iron, usually to his advantage. People described him as a cruel, nasty person with a sadistic streak and a natural bully who made his wife's life miserable.

Up to the beginning of December 1857, Barbara Sagar was in good health. She had complained of a bad leg, but that had healed, and she continued with her duties as workhouse matron. However, from the 12th December 1857, her health deteriorated, and her doctor confined her to bed. Friends called on her, and Barbara complained to them that she had a terrible burning sensation in her stomach, and she was constantly sick and thirsty. She said to her friend Mrs Smith that she would die, upon which her husband remarked 'that she had said this so many times, that she best makes haste about it.' Her husband placed a clean cover on the bed, which Mrs Sagar told him to remove as he would need it soon enough to lay her out.

Barbara Sagar was very wary of the medicine her husband gave her, so much so that she said to Mrs Bland of the Keighley Union, 'take that bottle and smash it to shivers, as I will take no more of it, it will kill me.' John Sagar was there when she said this, so at his wife's and Mrs Bland's request, he went downstairs and returned around two hours later with what he said was a new bottle with the name 'Julep' on it. He persuaded her to take another dose, she did, but shortly after, she threw her arms in the air, declaring that she was going to die.

Mary Ann Scarborough, Barbara's sister, was present, and knowing her sister's dislike of medicine, bravely took downstairs two bottles and tested one with no ill effect. 'It's not that bottle that gives me pain. It's the other one with the name on it.' Her ailing sister declared. Barbara's symptoms and pain continued, and on Saturday 19th December 1857, she was found dead in her bed curled in a foetal position, her fists clenched, her tongue protruding with a look of unbearable pain on her face. Unaccountably, the Julep bottle had conveniently disappeared.

The funeral took place the following Wednesday, but rumours began circulating the town about how the master of the workhouse ill-treated his wife. These rumours, which included statements saying that Barbara had told her friends that her husband was trying to poison her, and in the week before, she'd said 'if owt 'appens to me, then you might think it was murder.' These rumours and accusations reached the attention of the County Coroner, Mr Thomas Brown of Skipton. He decided to stop the internment and instructed surgeon Mr Ruddick of Keighley to conduct a post-mortem examination of the body.

Mr Ruddick, in conjunction with Mr Ainley of Bingley, carried out a post-mortem examination and afterwards, he sent the intestines, kidneys and rectum to Mr Morley, surgeon of Leeds, for chemical analysis, requesting the results to be returned to Mr Ruddick by letter.

An inquest opened the same day at The Crown Inn, Keighley, but this inquest adjourned until the following Saturday after a lengthy examination. Mr Ruddick produced the required letter, which caused a sensation as his analysis proving the presence of arsenic in Barbara Sagar's body was enough to have caused her death. Unfortunately, for legal reasons, this letter was not accepted as evidence.

Rumours did not diminish, with every aspect of the Sagar's life dissected. Quickly, tales spread about how Sagar treated his wife; by all accounts, John was a cruel, brutal man. He had a mistress, and he had tortured his wife both physically and mentally for many years. He had locked Barbara in the 'dead house' (workhouse mortuary) and beat her on one occasion. Another time one of the female inmates named Mitchell found Barbara handcuffed and chained to her bed to neither sit, stand, nor lie down. John Sagar later said she deserved this punishment as she had mistreated some of the workhouse children.

Following up on the various rumours circulating regarding the maltreatment of Mrs Sagar, John Cheeseborough, the Chief Superintendent of Keighley, went to Exley Head Workhouse to do a search and interview John Sagar. He had heard rumours that Sagar was dealing in the sale of arsenic and that there were many more dubious dealings within the dirty walls of the workhouse. In a cupboard, he found two bottles with different coloured powders. Sagar became agitated, took one bottle, and attempted to shake the contents onto the floor. The superintendent managed to grab his hand to stop him and put the remains of the bottle into a paper bag to send for analysis. It was then that Superintendent Cheeseborough arrested Sagar and took him into custody.

The following Tuesday, crowds of people flocked to the courthouse for the trial, anticipating that Sagar would appear at the Crown Inn for the inquest. Still, they were disappointed as the Coroner had adjourned the hearing and moved it to the nearby courthouse. Nevertheless, in a noticeably short time, the area was full of females wanting to see the prisoner.

John Sagar was brought to the court handcuffed to the officials; the papers described him as 'a a dirty, repulsive man with his left hand missing.' The charges against him had a considerable effect on Sagar's health. A miserable and sad man, broken in spirit, he had refused to eat while in the lock-up. He was so miserable. He cried in his sleep. The officers were concerned about his health and put him on suicide watch. He shook profoundly through fear – or perhaps guilt while being questioned and cried throughout much of the hearing.

Numerous witnesses came forward to state their side of the story, with various accounts of the husband's ill-treatment with his wife. The sister of the prisoner, Hannah Sagar, gave her evidence to say that she had been with her sister-in-law on the day she died and the week before her death. 'Barbara had suffered from sickness all week. Doctor Milligan called on her and later sent her a bottle of medicine. My brother had been attentive to his wife and called on her at regular intervals. He gave her I sat up with her all night, and she got worse. Finally, on Saturday morning, around four o'clock, I noticed she had turned around and breathed slowly. I called my brother; he came into the room, and Barbara died soon after.' a teaspoonful of the medicine, and Barbara vomited.

John Milligan, district medical officer for the Keighley Union, attended the deceased before her death. In his opinion, he had not considered Mrs Sagar to be seriously ill. Thus he had prescribed her a bottle of saline solution. His diagnosis was that she was suffering from a bilious attack. He had seen her again the Wednesday before her death. She refused to take any more of that 'stuff', meaning the medicine. Her husband took the bottle away and said he would bring her some fresh. When her husband went downstairs, she vomited and  said  to him, 'he has killed me – I'm going to die!' Mrs Bland was in the room when she witnessed the deceased's outcry of 'he's put poison  in the – he is killing me.' At the magistrate's inquest, he concluded that Mrs Sagar had died because of inflammation of the stomach caused by poisoning.

Keighley surgeon William Ruddick deposed that he had carried out the post-mortem, externally there were signs of discolouration of the skin around the hips and loins. Most likely caused by blows at different times. Furthermore, there were blisters on her chest and excessive inflammation in the bowels and rectum.

George Morley, a surgeon of Leeds, confirmed that he did not doubt the presence of arsenic in the samples he received. He wasn't wrong. After analysing the samples, he found two and a half grams of arsenic – more than enough to kill the lady, and in his opinion, arsenic poisoning was the cause of death. Then, insensitively, the Coroner made the statement, 'Isn't there a degree of arsenic in every human body?'

'Not in all', responded the eminent surgeon, but in this case, I have found enough arsenic in Mrs Sagar's body to destroy her life. Arguments continued that perhaps Mrs Sagar took the arsenic externally to relieve Mrs Sagar's bad leg symptoms, and perhaps, the arsenic had been absorbed through the skin and into the stomach and intestines. Mr Morley quickly disagreed with this hypothesis.

The following person to give evidence caused such a shock and sensation that even the press considered her statement 'too disgusting for publication'. Ann Bland was the twenty-two-year-old unmarried daughter of Thomas and Martha Bland, who worked for the poor house union. The whole courtroom was silent as Ann gave her testimony. People suspected that Ann was the 'other woman' in John Sagar's life. When asked if this rumour was true, Ann admitted, 'yes, it was true.' Nobody expected what she was to say next. She alleged that Mrs Sagar encouraged this relationship between her husband and this young girl. The couple enticed her into conducting an affair with both Mr and Mrs Sagar. Four years earlier, when Ann was only eighteen. Barbara asked Ann to go to bed with her. She also told her 'not to be afraid of her husband if he came and joined them as well as a threesome.' It was at this time she had improper intercourse with the prisoner, who had taken her virtue. Ann said she had slept with the couple many times since. She had also witnessed her sister Martha Wadsworth sleep with Sagar and his wife. An allegation that was Mrs Wadsworth vehemently denied. – A shocked Mrs Wadsworth declared the allegation untrue and downright disgusting.

Ann was not the only member of the Bland family to disgrace herself. Her father, Thomas Bland, one of the guardians responsible for running the workhouse, was censored by the judge for perjury by writing a personal letter to the judge to stop his wife from giving evidence. The judge did not take kindly to this and made his feelings on this attempt to pervert the course of justice known. Bland then refused to answer any questions asked of him. Irritated, the judge gave Bland some strong words from the bench. 'It is obvious to me that you have committed the grossest perjury in the witness box, which is clear for all to hear. You leave this court a disgraced man. It is clear to me that you are trying to screen this murder and that there is a vast conspiracy to conceal the prisoner John Sagar's murderous intentions.'

One witness from the workhouse stated that the prisoner's sister Hannah Sagar had warned the inmates not to testify and not under any circumstances to talk about bottles or anything that went on in the workhouse. Martha Bland, the wife of Thomas and mother of Ann, said she knew that Mr Sagar was poisoning his wife, and there was plenty more she knew, but she would never tell. She knew that there was a bottle labelled Julep, which had conveniently disappeared.

This evidence concluded the enquiry. Subsequently, John Sagar was charged with the murder of his wife and committed to York Castle to await trial at the assizes.

The trial began in March 1858. Acting for the prosecution was Mr Foster, Mr Maule, and Mr West. Defending the prisoner was Mr Digby Seymour and Mr Dearsley. The presiding judge was Mr Justice Byles.

A dishevelled looking Sagar was brought up and asked how he pleaded. In a broken, tearful voice, he said, 'not guilty'.

However, from the start, matters did not bode well for the prosecution. First, the judge ruled that the evidence of Ann Bland, which had caused such a sensation at the magistrate's enquiry, was inadmissible since her relationship with John Sagar had taken place with the consent of his wife. This revelation was despite the considerable evidence that John Sagar and Ann Bland had clandestine extramarital relations outside of Sagar's marriage without Barbara Sagar's knowledge. Their adultery could well have been a motive for murder.

Moreover, causing an outcry from around the courtroom, Sagar's previous cruelty to his wife was also considered inadmissible. Despite witnesses testifying, Sagar grabbed his wife from her bed by her hair and kicked her in the stomach.

Further witnesses gave their account of the Sagars' life. Many were confirming they had seen Sagar administering medicine to his wife. They further demonstrated that she complained of thirst and a burning in her throat after taking it, followed by hours of vomiting. She died soon after.

The crux of the trial came when inexplicably, John Milligan, workhouse surgeon, changed his testimony from what he initially said in the Coroner's inquest. He deposed that he had attended Mrs Sagar during her illness and that he saw no symptoms under which the deceased laboured, which led him to believe that she had taken arsenic. In his opinion, Barbara Sagar had died from inflammation of the stomach caused by spontaneous causes.

With that admission, Mr Foster announced that his learned colleagues in the prosecution agreed with him and that they ought not to proceed further with this case. He felt bound to say that 'witnesses' had not given such evidence that day in support of this case as they had at the first inquest. At the same time, the jury was obliged to consider the evidence as it appeared to them and feeling as he did – the evidence presented would not secure a conviction. Therefore, he proposed the prosecution, and with His Lordship's sanction, he respectfully asked to retire from this prosecution.

His Lordship responded, 'I think you have acted perfectly proper in the circumstances.'

Addressing the jury, His Lordship said, 'the medical man, in this case, has sworn that the death had arisen from natural causes. But, on the other hand, there has been evidence given of cruelty, which is most disgraceful but cannot prejudice the prisoner in this matter, and I tell the jury that they should not pay the slightest attention to it! – Besides this, it is usual in evidence that the poisoning symptoms from arsenic are present, 'burning and sickness' for ten minutes to half an hour after Mrs Sagar too the poison. However, in this case, I have seen no evidence that this was the case within this time frame. Therefore, I think it would never be easy in your minds to take a life on such sparse evidence as this – and you will best discharge your duty by returning a verdict of not guilty.'

Accordingly, taking His Lordship's comments into account, and based on the evidence put before them, the jury found a verdict of 'Not Guilty.'

Sagar was discharged of all charges and walked away from court a free man.

* * *

The public was outraged over this whole case, and they did not want to accept the verdict, yet they had no choice. Still, questions should be asked - especially of Milligan – why did he change his statement from the inquest to the trial? Why was he persuaded to do so, if so, for what reason? Did he know too much? Was he defending Sagar as Milligan himself played a principal role in Barbara Sagar's death? Was it he who administered the poison to his patient? Perhaps there was some terrible hold Sagar had over him to make him change his statement in such a dramatic way? Perhaps both men were part of a secret pact – all questions which there are no answers. Milligan received criticism for his actions during and after the trial, and he and Surgeon George Morley conducted a war of words in the newspaper 'The Leeds Intelligencer. George Morley having more experience and medical knowledge, came across as the superior doctor and concluded that Milligan had no medical reason for his sudden change of opinion that altered the outcome of the prosecution.

Did Barbara receive the justice she deserved? A significant amount of arsenic was found in her body after her death, as Mr Morley observed 'enough to cause death.' There was evidence of previous violence and brutality; her husband had a continuing relationship with another woman, albeit initially with his wife's consent. Barbara was sure that her husband was trying to kill her – did a murderer escape the scaffold – unfortunately, we will never know.

John Sagar moved to Bradford and went back to his previous profession as a painter. He remarried to a lady named Elizabeth, twenty-two years his junior. The couple lived quietly at 45 White Abbey Road, Bradford. John died in 1873, aged 69.

R.I.P Barbara Sagar.

# CHAPTER 4

# 1872. Crompton Nr Pickering. Murder & Mutilation Joseph Wood & His Son Joseph Thompson.

*No one to help them, no one to save*
*No one but heaven to point out their grave*
*The poor man and boy would have done him no harm.*
*Were murdered by Charter at Cropton Lane Farm.*

Four miles from Pickering and about half a mile from Crompton Village is Cropton Lane, when in 1872 stood a farm owned by Joseph Wood. For generations, the Wood family had farmed the eighty acres. Joseph was the eldest of ten children born to Joseph and Anne Wood; he inherited the farm following the death of his parents. At that time, four brothers and three sisters were still living.

Joseph lived at the farm with his two sons, five-year-old Thomas and nine-year-old Joseph, and his eighteen-year-old daughter Charlotte Ann Thompson. All the children were illegitimate and were born to Joseph's housekeeper Catherine Thompson, who died in October 1871. The children all took their mother's surname and not their father's.

Fifty-eight-year-old Joseph had occupied the farm for thirty-seven years. An eccentric, odd man, yet Joseph was known as a hard-headed Yorkshireman, a good farmer, and a friendly neighbour who was generally well-liked throughout the neighbourhood. The villagers used to laugh at his peculiarities, and now and then, they would wind him up and provoke him – just for the fun of it. Money was his nemesis. Sometimes he would pay his suppliers nothing until they sued him, whilst on other occasions, he would insist on paying twice the invoice amount. His housekeeper and partner kept him going, but after her death, he went to pieces. Initially, Joseph's daughter Charlotte took on the role of housekeeper, but it was all too much for her to handle on her own. Her father refused to get her any help, so she left and lived with her grandparents. Joseph took to keeping large amounts of cash, gold, and silver in the farmhouse, which was well-known throughout the village.

Joseph and his brother John, who lived further down the road with a farm of his own, were reasonably close with the rest of his family. Robert Charter, the family's cousin, and himself a small farmer lived three miles away in Lastingham with his wife Hannah and three adult children: Martha, 30, Sarah, 28, and John, 26. Charter's son-in-law William Hardwick sometimes helped Charter on his farm.

On occasions, Charter helped Joseph with Cropton Lane Farm, as he did on Friday 17th May 1872 when he travelled to Wood's farm with a wagon load of seed barley in readiness for sowing. However, it seems that the men must have had a disagreement as Joseph and his nine-year-old son Joseph Thompson disappeared.

John Wood told the police that he last saw his brother on 7th May sat in front of his kitchen fire with his two children. He was well and not in an agitated state. He could be doolally at times; the family had been worried about him and even considered having him committed to the

Asylum as he would not get on with his work, and he refused to pay his taxes. John told the police he saw Robert Charter the following day, saying, 'I take it the master has gone away and taken young Joseph with him.' John said he was puzzled. His brother did not mention that he was going away, and he thought it was extraordinary that he would do so without telling the family. John asked Charter where his brother had gone? Charter replied he didn't know and that he didn't feel that it was his business to ask. He said, 'he just waved at me as he left and told me to stay at the farm and to look after things for him.' John was suspicious; to him, something was just not quite right.

The following week a letter arrived from Liverpool purporting to have been written by Joseph Wood. The letter said,

Liverpool – May 20, 1872. To
Robert Charter,


Dear Cousin,
I write these few lines to let you know that I will take the water, foreign; You must stop at Croft-Lane and get my affairs settled as soon as you can. We are going either today or tomorrow. I will let you know in my heart what I have done and where I am going. Excuse my bad writing, a bad pen and in haste.
Joseph Wood.


To corroborate this letter, he showed it to John Wood, who was sceptical about its authenticity. Curious, John pointed out to Charter that it was strange that the postmark on the letter was the 22 May. Yet Joseph states he wrote on 20th his intention to go abroad, either on that day or the 21st.

Charter responded, 'perhaps he got the date wrong?'

This letter was not in Joseph's handwriting, but extraordinarily, except for John, the rest of the family believed their brother's intentions.

A short time after this, Charter moved his wife into Cropton Lane Farm and some of his farming stock. However, his wife was not happy and did not feel comfortable on the farm, so she returned to her own home after only one month. Except for Charter, nobody slept at the farmhouse. The labourers had their meals there but returned to their own homes each evening.

Four months passed, and Charter left the farm and returned to his smallholding in Lastingham. Joseph Wood and his son had not returned. John was still not convinced that his brother had simply up and left, so he decided to search the barns. On clearing a bale of straw, some clothing items and a pair of Joseph's boots fell out. John undertook a further search of the farmhouse and found another pair of boots under the stairs. John knew that his brother did not own any more boots. He also found a jacket and a waistcoat belonging to his young nephew Joseph.

With his doubts confirmed, John informed the police of his findings and his suspicions about the inexplicable disappearance of his brother.

Sergeant Jonas of Pickering ordered a full investigation, starting with a thorough search of the farmhouse and outbuildings. Finding nothing, they moved on to a pool in the pasture. They were not searching for long when they saw some items of clothing. The following day the pond was dredged, and more clothing found. Next, a muddy deposit was removed, which revealed a human left hand found sticking out of the mud. Next, police found a mouth-brace, then two human feet and a clenched hand with a straw in its firm grip.

Jonas and Inspector Pickering of Thirsk travelled to Lastingham to search the fields farmed by Charter. Police search all six fields and found nothing. They next crossed the road and searched a recently ploughed field; they saw an old watercourse covered with fresh soil at the bottom of this field. A little further down, they found a three-pronged fork, a spade, and a plough. The police dug down to a depth of two and a half feet, where they found many stones recently put there. On further investigation, police found a stack of rocks in the corner of the field, from which there was a large hole. They removed the stones to around three and a half feet, where Jonas found a sack – on closer inspection, he saw a bone protruding which later proved to be the knee of the murdered man.

At this point, the police arrested Charter for the murder of Joseph Wood.

There is a beck close to Charter's farm. Police searched the beck and discovered a sack, which contained the remains of Joseph Wood minus his hands and feet. Tied firmly around his neck was a rope. Body flesh was still attached to his body. It seems before he left Wood's farm, Charter buried Wood's body in an orchard and in a hurry to remove the corpse, the feet were left behind – complete with stockings. A woman who darned Wood's socks confirmed they were his as she recognised her stitching.

Investigators completed an examination of what remained of the body found in the sack. Although whiskers remained and some hair, the body was severely decomposed, later identified as belonging to Mr Joseph Wood. The temporal bone on the left side, the facial bone, the nasal bone, and his teeth were either broken or missing. Most likely from being struck over the head with some blunt instrument, then, to ensure that he was dead. The discovery of straw found on the body confirmed that the murder took place in the barn. John Wood stated that his brother was a compulsive smoker and had black teeth. On examination, the teeth were found to be a maroon colour and heavily stained with nicotine.

Unfortunately, the only remains of young Joseph were his shoes found in the boiler room at Cropton Farm and threads of his trousers found in a turnip field. This boiler room was housed in a small building in the yard and used for chiefly boiling food for cattle. The discovery of young Joseph's shoes gave rise to the suspicion that the murderer used this room to dispose of the body, which he then fed to the pigs.

An initial inquest into the murders took place at The Horseshoe Inn Pickering on Saturday, 23rd November 1872, in front of Mr John Ness, North Riding Coroner and deputy coroner Dr Wood. The prisoner Robert Charter was not present as he was unwell and considered too unfit to attend. By all accounts, he was suffering from deep depression and unable to walk unaided.

The deceased's brothers William and John Wood identified the remains and Charlotte Thompson, Wood's illegitimate daughter.

The jury read two statements written by Charter whilst on remand. In the first, he states that on 17th May, he heard a noise and went out of the house to see what was happening when he saw Joseph Wood lying dead against a wall, covered in blood. He feared he would be accused of his death, so Charter took him into the barn and put him in the straw. He then foddered the cattle. Charter kept the body in the barn for a week. He then buried the body under a heap in the orchard. About three weeks later, Charter found some small bones in the yard, which Charter thought were those of the missing boy, which seemed pigs had gnawed. He buried these bones next to his father. Charter left the body in the orchard until a week before he left the farm. He tried to pull the body from the grave when all the clothes fell off, which he threw into a pond. Then he put the body in a bag and buried it near the beck at Lastingham. He then wrote a letter and gave it to a boy to post who said he would post it from Liverpool. Charter thought this course of action would prevent 'so much trouble in rowing and searching about till things got settled.'

In his second statement, he admits that he argued with his cousin over barley that Charter had brought to Cropton Lane Farm. Still, his cousin demanded he takes it back immediately for reasons unknown. The deceased presented a gun at him, so Charter followed him into the garden, where he picked up an iron instrument from the wall and struck Joseph Wood over the head with it. He did not intend to kill him – he did not think he had flogged him as to kill him. Charter also stated that he'd not see the boy at all. He admitted to burying Joseph's body in the centre of the field at his farm at Lastingham.

William Hardwick charged with being an accessory after the fact. At the close of this first inquiry, the jury found him guilty of wilful murder. Both men would now face trial at York Castle.

A grand jury dropped all charges regarding the disappearance and alleged murder of the boy. The only evidence connected with his disappearance was the discovery amongst some manure of some bones believed to be his. It was assumed the remainder of his body had been most revoltingly, devoured by pigs. There was, however, no definite medical determination that the bones belonged to him.

The three-day trial began on 25th March 1873. Fifty-three-year-old Charter and his son in law thirty-seven-year-old WM Hardwick opened at York Castle. Public interest in the case was high. People were fascinated as to the different ways the prisoner had tried to dispose of his cousin's body.

A large crowd gathered at the castle gates, all wanting to gain admittance to the proceedings. Many were disappointed.

Mr Maule QC (Recorder for Leeds) and Mr Simpson (Recorder for Scarborough) presented the case for the prosecution, and Mr Digby Seymour QC and Mr Waddy were for the defence.

When the prisoners appeared before the dock, they were pale and nervous. Charter, the taller man, was slender in stature with iron-grey hair and whiskers of a darker colour. Hardwick was more petite, better dressed and appeared to be far superior in intelligence. All eyes were on them as Mr Maule opened proceedings, putting forward the facts of the case. When the prisoners answered both the defence and the prosecution questions, both men spoke in low distinct voices and pleaded 'Not Guilty.'

The deceased's brother John Wood gave evidence to say that his brother had a good relationship with Robert Charter. Joseph was a good farmer, but he had strange ways. For some reason, he would not pay his taxes, and recently, the bailiffs seized some of his sheep under a distress warrant, but brother, Thomas Wood, had found the money to have the sheep released. Joseph owned his farm outright and had gold, silver, and watches in the house.

Superintendent Jonas of Pickering police produced several items of clothing belonging to the deceased found in the pond and different parts of the house. On 6th November, Jonas went to Charter's house to tell him that he believed Charter had murdered Mr Wood. Charter replied, 'It's a bad job. I heard when I was in Helmsley that you'd found some bits of clothing. The following day Jonas said that on Cropton Lane buried in an orchard, he found a human right hand and two feet which still had stockings on with the toes upward. Jonas arrested Charter for murder, but Charter still proclaimed his innocence. Jonas confirmed that he found writing paper and envelopes like the letter received from Liverpool allegedly written by Joseph Wood on searching Charter's house.

William Hardwick was taken into custody and charged with being an accessory after the fact.

Charlotte Ann Thompson, the daughter of the deceased, identified her father's clothing. Several witnesses gave evidence confirming that they saw Charter and Hardwick working together in a field near the beck where they found the body. Another witness Thomas Normington swore he saw both men as he passed the spot where they found the body. However, this witness had previously told Sergeant Jonas that he could swear he saw Charter, but he was not definite about Hardwick. His Lordship was far from impressed with this witness, and he rebuked him for his evasiveness and made two different statements on such an important matter. This evidence concluded on the first day of the trial.

On the second day of the trial public interest in the case had not diminished, and the courtroom was once more crowded.

Mr Maude, for the prosecution, proposed to call witnesses to prove that a search had made for the missing son of the deceased, who had most likely been the only witness to the murder. Still, despite a search, only some tiny bones were found that were not identified as belonging to the boy.

Mr Seymour objected, pointing out that Charter faced no charges for the boy's murder. Maude pointed out that it was necessary to produce some corroborative evidence on this part of the case. The prosecution asked the question as to whether Supt Jonas purposely searched for the boy's body or accidentally or intentionally altered Charter's statement regarding the words 'the three bones of the boy'. The judge said he would receive the evidence but would probably review it at a later stage.

Thomas Berriman, a labourer, gave his evidence that when he was working at Cropton Lane Farm, he took manure from the foldyard adjacent to the pigsty and placed it in heaps on the field. In turning over the heaps, he found a bone he believed to be human, so he gave it to the police.

Surgeon JH Walker gave evidence confirming he had examined the deceased's body; he inspected the skull and found a deep wound, most likely struck with a heavy instrument as the wound penetrated the whole skull. This blow to the head was sufficient to cause death. He had also examined the three bones of the boy and confirmed that they were indeed human and belonged to a child aged 8-10.

The judge asked the witness if there could be any other reason for the deceased's death except for a blow. The witness replied, 'No'.

This evidence concluded the case for the prosecution. At this time, Mr Waddy submitted with regards to WM Hardwick that there was no case to put before the jury to him being an accessory to the murder.

Mr Digby Seymour addressed the jury for the defence of Mr Charter; he reminded the jury that the prisoner was not on trial for the murder of the boy, and they should ignore this aspect of the case. The law had said there was no *prima facie* case to answer regarding the boy's death. Seymour further argued that there was no doubt there had been some quarrel between the couple, but there was no deliberate attempt at murder and no motive for murder.

In summing up, the judge said that the matter had been investigated, and the case was clear and straightforward. Mr Wood and his son had disappeared and his whereabouts a mystery for several months. Then parts of his body turned up in various parts of Yorkshire. Suspicion fell on Charter. His Lordship stressed to the jury that they were not to try Charter for the murder of the boy. There was no indictment for that. The prisoner Charter has admitted that he struck Wood with an iron on the back of his head, but there was no malice aforethought and no premeditation of killing him. If the jury agreed with this, it would be their duty to reduce their verdict to manslaughter, but that decision must be based on the evidence.

A great deal of weight provided by counsel on behalf of Charter was that there was no motive for murder. However, to cover up the death of his cousin, he resorted to falsehood, and he unquestionably forged a letter he alleged to be written by the deceased. He arranged for the delivery of this letter from Liverpool.

Concerning Hardwick, before the jury could find him guilty, they needed to be satisfied that he was aware his father-in-law Charter had committed a murder or manslaughter and that he helped him to conceal it.

The jury was absent for forty minutes. Then, finally, the Clerk of Arraigns asked, 'Gentlemen of the jury, are you all agreed?'

Foreman replied, 'yes.'

'Do you find the prisoner Robert Charter guilty or not guilty of wilful murder?'

'Not guilty.'

This announcement produced looks of amazement, shock, and astonishment from around the courtroom. A couple of the jury members had a glimpse of discord on their faces.

The foreman then asked, 'Do you find Robert Charter guilty of manslaughter?'

'Guilty of manslaughter.'

'Do you find the prisoner William Hardwick guilty or not guilty?'

'Not guilty as an accessory to either murder or manslaughter.'

Addressing Robert Charter, His Lordship said, 'Robert Charter, you have been found guilty of the serious crime of manslaughter. Have you anything to say as to why I should not pass sentence upon you.'

Scratching his head, Charter said in a low voice. 'I have done innocently what I did.'

The Lord Justice spoke directly to Charter.

'You have been found guilty of manslaughter. However, there are circumstances connected with this case that are extraordinary. You asserted two violent blows with a heavy instrument which caused the death of the deceased. You spread false reports of Mr Wood's disappearance, including sending a letter proclaiming to be from the dead man – to deceive his relatives. In disposing of the body, your conduct is all circumstances that seriously aggravate the offence you have been found guilty of. The sentence of this court is that you receive Penal Servitude for twenty years.'

* * *

Charter spent most of his sentence at Parkhurst Prison on the Isle of Wight. He was released early from his sentence and returned to Yorkshire, but there was nothing left for him in Lastingham. A sale of his property took place at auction in February 1876. The property consisted of a house, an orchard, two cottages and three closes of land.

The Darley family bought the property, and the villagers demolished the house stone by stone. In its place, they built a village school named The Darley Memorial School. In 1946, the Darley family gave the building to the town, and the property is now Lastingham Village Hall. Joseph Wood and Joseph Thompson are buried in Cropton churchyard.

May they both rest in peace.

* * *

# CHAPTER 5

## 1889. Sherburn In Elmet. The Savage Murder – George Mountain.

*Finkle Hill (High Street) – Sherburn in Elmet 1891*

In 1889, widow Catherine Mountain, a respectable, well-to-do woman, ran The Travellers Rest, a small public house on Finkle Hill adjoining the grammar school, on the main thoroughfare in the quiet village of Sherburn in Elmet near Selby. Catherine's husband had died twenty years earlier; the couple had four children, three boys and one girl. Sadly, all the children died except for thirty-four-year-old George. Mrs Mountain had an eight-year-old grandson named Willie, the only child of her deceased daughter. Catherine had not been seen around the village for a while on account of her ill-health and infirmity.

George served an apprenticeship in Selby as a grocer, but he had lived with his mother at the pub acting as her manager for the last twelve-fourteen years. George was well-liked in the village and known as a hard-working man with a quiet, gentle disposition – 'he wouldn't hurt a fly' was the consensus. Recently George had become engaged to a young lady from Horsforth, the wedding arranged for November 1889.  A few days previously to events, George discussed his forthcoming marriage with the local shopkeepers; his mother opposed the wedding. Nevertheless, George insisted that he would still be looking after his mother after his wedding and making her life comfortable. Although a genial chap, concerns for George's mental health was growing amongst his family and friends. Although he was a 'lovely man, his personality completely changed with alcohol when he became ungovernable. Six months previously, after a continuous drinking bout, he had left the pub in the middle of the night and roused the whole village from their sleep, running up and down the main road shouting 'murder, murder', and generally causing a commotion. The police were called but didn't consider his actions at the time too severe and that once he sobered up, he would be fine. However, they did insist that a couple of strong men watch over him at the pub for a couple of months, and they took away his revolver as a precaution. Ironically, the police gave him his gun back two days before the incident.

Servant girl Annie Hutchinson, who was of Scottish heritage, lived in the pub and had worked for Mrs Mountain for five years. On Wednesday evening, 10th October 1889, George was working behind the bar. Once again, he was inebriated and had been drinking steadily for the last few days while consuming little food. Finally, around ten in the evening, George called last orders, and the pub closed. Grandson Willie was fast asleep in bed. His grandmother was in the habit of locking the child's door when the pub was open but unlocked it when the pub closed for the evening.

At ten o'clock, all customers had left. Annie was in the bar washing glasses, Catherine Mountain was in her private apartment known as the 'top room'. After locking the outer door, George went upstairs to the top room, and as he passed the door at the bottom of the stairs, he shut it. Fifteen minutes later, he went back down to the bar and pulled himself another pint of beer. Annie observed him, George had had too much alcohol, having drunk steadily on beer and whisky for the previous few days. Annie had seen him worse. His face had a wild look to it, but he was walking straight, and he could speak. Still, she knew him well enough to know something was very wrong. When she had finished washing the glasses, she sat down at the bar. George called out to her, 'have you finished washing the glasses?'

'Yes,' she replied.

'So, turn the gas out, lock the door and bring the key up to the top room.'

This was an unusual request, as usually, he was the one to lock up, but Annie didn't quibble and did as he asked. She found George and his mother sitting on the sofa in the top room next to the fire. Annie gave him the key, and he put it in his pocket.

George was agitated and stood up; he went over to the room door and locked it. 'You will be stopping up all night!' he bellowed, 'If I'd known that, I would have got myself a few nuts to crack.' Then, taking a handful of walnuts from his pockets, he threw them at her.

'Can I have the key please?' said Annie.

'No, I told you I would not give the key up. That door will not open tonight.'

George crossed the room impatiently and took a pistol from a cabinet and loaded it. 'Don't worry, Annie,' said Mrs Mountain, 'he isn't going to use it. He only wants to frighten us; one of his 'silly' nights again!' Annie sighed, she had witnessed George in this state before, and at this time, she wasn't so concerned, so she went to join Mrs Mountain on the sofa, each sitting at opposite ends.

George retorted, 'You wait and see what I am going to do!' He then sat down. Wild and distressed, he stood up again, ranting, 'She is not my mother, that woman lying on the sofa, look at her, look at her, that's not my mother.' Now scared, Catherine Mountain tried to soothe her disturbed son. Anxious, she tried to hold his hand, repeatedly reassuring him that yes, of course, she was his mother. George was not convinced and shouted at her, 'No, you are not, you are too old!' At this, he pulled the jacket off her shoulders and demanded that she take off her clothes. 'You look nothing like my mother, nothing at all.' Annie stood up, trying to defend her mistress, but George pushed her out of the way and pushed his mother onto the floor. Turning back to Annie, he yelled at her wildly, 'There are only you two, what have you come here to do?.

I don't mind which one of you I do first!'

Bravely, Mrs Mountain stood up and squared up to her son, 'You are not going to do either of us; if you do, then you will not live long afterwards!' Then, pushing her back down to the floor, he again yelled at her, 'Shut up, you are not my mother, you and she are coming to do me, I know what this is all about!'

For months, George had got it into his head that someone was coming to get him; he became paranoid about it, and the drink didn't help. Then, at that moment, George snapped, he struck his mother with force across the forehead with his fist, and she fell to the floor.

Alarmed, Annie rushed to grab the poker from the fireplace; she was no match for the surly George who snatched it out of her hand. Annie ran to the window and tried desperately to open the shutters. George rushed at her with fury and vitriol before grabbing her hands and throwing her to the floor. 'If you try to open those shutters or move from that spot again, I will shoot you!' At this, Catherine tried once more to get up from the floor, but George flipped, saw red and tore all his mother's clothes off, kicking her brutally in her head and about her body. For a few hours, George continued to kick her intermittently. The poor frail woman was helpless and moaned in pain for hours. At one time, George dragged his mother roughly across the floor then continued to kick and punch her repeatedly brutally. Afterwards, he turned to Annie, and said 'How long have you been here? How did you get in? It's your turn next; you can lie down on the floor beside your mate.' Knowing the situation was inevitable, Annie thought it best to keep quiet; there was nothing more she could do. Finally, around seven-thirty in the morning, George took out the screw to the window and opened the shutters. Annie glimpsed through the window and saw a man she recognised, Mr Joseph Johnson, walking past. Grabbing the opportunity, she ran to the window and yelled for help at the top of her voice. Johnson came to see what all the commotion was about and climbed through the window, horrified at the scene that greeted him. He took the pistol away from George's hand, which he had gripped throughout the night. A hysterical Annie managed to blurt out the words, 'he's killed her, he's killed his mother!'

Still, in denial, a bewildered George said, 'She's not my mother.'

Mr Lofthouse, seen walking past, was called into the house. But, like Johnson, he could not believe the barbarity of the scene and ran off to fetch the police.

Shortly after, Inspector Towler arrived and placed George Mountain under arrest. Annie was questioned and confirmed that she had never seen him threaten or raise a cross word to his mother. However, it transpired that not only had he kicked his mother, he had also stamped viciously on her face and stabbed her in her side with a penknife, which he had in his pocket.

The surgeon, Joseph Thirkell, called at eight-thirty Thursday morning and, like the police, were horrified by what he saw. Mrs Mountain was lying on the floor of the top room. He examined the body and found that the poor old lady had two broken legs, her face mutilated, and her features unrecognisable.

He carried out a post-mortem. Mrs Mountain had a deep laceration wound on her right forearm, and she had several large bruises on her limbs and body. The lower jaw smashed to pieces, the skin and bone were missing, and the upper jaw had disappeared entirely. Both eyes were hanging out of their sockets. The scalp separated from the bone, her right collar bone broken, her ribs broken, one of which was penetrating her lung. Her liver was ruptured and reduced to a pulp. In the doctor's opinion, death primarily had occurred due to a concussion of the brain.

In his report, Inspector Towler of the West Riding Constabulary said he was stationed at Sherburn when Mr Lofthouse ran into the station to report a murder at the Travellers Inn. He met with a horrific, bloody scene. As the door was not open, he went through the window, and the key could be found. Mountain, Johnson, and the maid were there. The body of Mrs Mountain was lying on the floor. Pieces of bone and flesh were everywhere. There was blood on the ceiling, floor, and walls. The Inspector arrested Mountain and charged him with the murder of his mother by kicking her to death. Now beginning to sober up, George said, 'I know what's done it, I have been too fond of money lately, but I did not think it was my mother. I thought it was someone else that the maid had brought in!' George was dazed and confused. His hands, trousers, and boots were all covered in blood. Horrifically, the officer saw hair and shattered bones in the fireplace. The policeman examined the pistol and found that it was loaded with gunpowder and shot, and there was a percussion cap on it.

George Mountain complained of pain in his head. The effects of the copious amount of beer, wine, whisky, and brandy he had consumed over the last few days were noticeable. He was confused, dazed, with a wild look on his face. Police Inspector Towler arrested him and took him into custody at Sherburn.

The following morning, word had quickly spread around the village; large crowds were assembling outside the Travellers Inn, all hoping for a glimpse into where this gruesome tragedy took place. Over the last twelve years, Sherburn had become a notorious place for violence. First, there had been a quarrel between two men in the street that had a fatal outcome. Then, another attempted murder by a man named Sissons happened in 1887, who had murdered a fellow prisoner at Armley Gaol. Now the murder of a mother by her only son.

Speculation was rife around the small town; despite the drink, the gossip was that George knew what he was doing, and the real reason he killed his mother was to get her out of the way. He wanted to get married, and his mother disapproved, so he murdered her. That way, the public house and his mother's fortune would then be his.

An inquest was opened at Sherburn the following day. The prisoner was brought before the judge and said, 'I didn't know what I was doing, I am not in my right mind. Can I see a doctor please, your honour?'

Annie was called as a witness. Still terrified, she retold the story of that frightful night, a night that would no doubt haunt her for life. She had, she said, been a prisoner in the house and forced to watch a crazed man brutally murder his mother in such a vile, obscene manner. The judge asked George what he had to say.

'No, your honour, I did not know what I was doing – I thought it was someone who had come to rob me, not my mother. I loved my mother!'

The police remanded George into custody for one week. Finally, on 15th December 1889, he appeared at the Leeds Assizes at Leeds Town Hall before Baron Pollock. In a quiet voice, George pleaded 'not guilty.'

Mr Banks and Mr CM Atkinson were for the prosecution and entered a plea of temporary insanity. Insanity had for generations plagued the Mountain family and was, it seemed, hereditary. George's afflictions were accentuated by a blow to the head he suffered two years previously. Dr Bevan Lewis, superintendent of Wakefield Asylum, examined George and gave evidence favouring his insanity plea. However, the judge stressed his concern that the jury is aware of this horrendous crime's circumstances. If it did transpire that alcohol, as suggested, reduced George's reasoning on a fateful day in question, then insanity would not be a defence at all. In the judge's opinion, alcohol was the 'curse of the land,' and any prisoner could not use the demon drink as an excuse for a crime. 'If as has been suggested that this prisoner carried out this vile act whilst not in possession of his faculties, then so be it, but it is the jury's job to decipher if he knew right from wrong at the time he committed this crime. The jury must be sure in their minds.'

After an absence of an hour, the jury returned a guilty verdict and found that the prisoner committed his crime whilst he was of unsound mind.

His Lordship then directed that the prisoner George Mountain retained at Her Majesty's Pleasure and sent to Broadmoor, where three years later, he died.

R.I. P Catherine Mountain.

## CRIMINAL INSANITY

Before 1806, asylums were privately run. An Act of 1808 provided funding for county asylums. Despite this financing, there were not many asylums built, and the 'criminally insane' tended to be kept in prisons and workhouses. People with means made their arrangements for mentally ill family members in private asylums. In 1845, the Lunacy Act and County Asylum Act obligated counties to build asylums for the poor and criminally insane.

Broadmoor Criminal Lunatic Asylum was built in 1868 on a three-hundred-acre site. Many prisoners were employed in the gardens, farms, carpenters' shops, and workshops if in a fit condition. A library and literacy lessons were also provided. Later, the 1890 Act gave asylums a more expansive role, and asylums admitted patients from a broad range of social classes.

*Broadmoor day room for male patients. © Wikimedia commons.*

# CHAPTER 6

## 1881. Holmfirth – Infanticide. The Triple Murders And Suicide. Hannah Moorhouse.

*Toss O Coin Inn. Formerly The Junction. © Toss O Coin Inn.*

**M**urder and suicides were unheard of in the tranquil *Last of the Summer Wine* village of Fulstone near Holmfirth, but one morning the residents of this close-knit community were shocked and sickened to discover a triple murder and a suicide had taken place close to the town.

Hannah Moorhouse, an unmarried mother of three, had drowned her three young children: Ada, aged 10, Emma Elizabeth 6, and 18-months-old Simeon John Hollingworth (known as John). As the story began to unfold, Hannah had planned the deaths of her children and returned to the crime scene three times.

Hannah lived with her mother Ann and stepfather Henry Battye, a farmer and the landlord of the Junction Inn, Syke Bottom, New Mill, Fulstone. (Now Toss O Coin Inn)

About noon on that fateful Tuesday morning, Henry had left home to go to Huddersfield Market. Before he left, he had had angry words with twenty-seven-year-old Hannah, and in his strong Yorkshire dialect, said, 'Dos't thou know what I mean when I talk, dos't thou understand me?' 'What about?' asked Hannah.

'Art thou in the family way?'

'No'

'Thou art? Well, thou may find a fresh shop a week from today, thou can take the bed, and ought that belongs to thee.'

Henry mentioned Hannah's eldest daughter Ada in the conversation. 'There is yon lass Ada. I have had to bring her up and educate her. Yet when she comes home from school. Thou do send her to work instead of letting her attend to her books!'

The atmosphere between the family must have been tense and most likely had been brewing for some time. A few days before, Hannah had packed three boxes and taken them to a neighbour's house, Mrs Barden's, without telling her family or her neighbour why.

No doubt, this conversation was the catalyst for the tragic events that followed. Perhaps Hannah was concerned that she would have nowhere for her and her children to live in a week, or maybe she wanted revenge on her parents. Nobody will ever know. Henry could not have imagined the dire consequences that this talk with his stepdaughter would bring.

Hannah's mother, Ann spoiled her daughter; Hannah could do no wrong in her eyes. Ann would give her daughter money and often the keys to the pub's money draw.  Hannah and her children had a free run of the house and were accustomed to getting anything they wanted when her mother was around. In return, Hannah did a little cleaning and a few chores around the inn.

Tragically, Hannah's brother John had been killed in a terrible accident two years previously whilst getting out of a train at Shepley. John had sat in a first-class train carriage with a third-class ticket. Avoiding  the ticket guard, he jumped from the train the wrong side of the carriage and hit by a passing train; his body not discovered until the following day Following the row with her father, Hannah had asked for her brother's box, which contained his trinkets and possessions, claiming her brother had given it to her at Honley Feast. Henry replied.

'If thou mother knows aught about it, thou can have it.'

Hannah did not let her troubles show by all accounts, but deep down, she must have been seething, plotting her deathly plan in her head. Yet, throughout that tragic day, she casually went about her chores cheerfully, even singing, whilst she attended the washing. The eldest Ada was at school whilst the younger children, Emma, and John played with bobbins on the tap-room table, blissfully unaware that this would be their last day on earth.

Hannah was a determined individual with a strong-willed personality. She did not give in easily and took most of her quick hot temper out on her mother. If Hannah did not get her way, she would go for weeks without speaking to anyone, and if anyone said a wrong word to her, then woe-betide. Before her death, she disagreed with her other brother, who had since moved to America, and she had not spoken to him for three months. If Hannah wanted to do something, nothing or no one could stop her.

Before her second child was born, Hannah had fallen out with her mother and moved out of the house. She wrote to her mother, calling her all the names under the sun. She also threatened to kill herself. Terrified, her mother wrote back to her and pacified matters. Hannah moved back home and had been there ever since. During this time, it seems that all was not well as Hannah had only spoken to her mother occasionally, and only then when she wanted something, or if she wanted to go out, asking her mother to mind her children.

Following school, a customer saw Ada coming down from the upstairs of the inn, doing her daily chores of emptying the slops. Hannah was ready to set her dreadful deathly plans in motion.

It is a complete mystery how Hannah persuaded Ada, her strapping ten-year-old daughter, to jump into a ten-foot-deep pond, set in a hollow belonging to Snowgate Head Coal Pit only 200 yards from the back of the inn where the family lived. Especially on a cold, wet December day, knowing that Ada could not swim and did not have a chance of climbing out of the bottomless pit; yet nobody heard a thing, there were no cries of help and no agonising final screams.

After Hannah was sure that her eldest child was dead, she returned to the inn to collect her younger children. Hannah was friendly with her neighbour Mrs Barden and went to her house with her two younger children. However, Mrs Barden was not at home, so she did not stay. Drayman George Hirst saw her next and recalled Hannah gripping her children's hands tightly as she walked along the wet road in the pouring rain in the pond's direction. He later remarked that he was surprised that none of them had bonnets on their heads despite it raining hard. He stopped to talk with Hannah, but she ignored him and continued to walk towards the pond.

On her second trip, it was middle child Emma's turn to be enticed to her death. The poor child must have been terrified as her mother persuaded her to jump. What is appalling is that the youngest child, John witnessed the end of his sister. Hopefully, he was too young to register that he would never see Emma again or the impact of the crime he had witnessed.

Incredibly, Hannah returned to the inn a third time, specifically to find her younger brother Henry working in the cowshed next to the inn. Her motive was to ensure that she had a messenger to relay the tragic deaths to her parents with maximum effect.

'Come along with me, I want you,' she said to her small brother. 'What for?' the young boy replied, as she marched off towards the dam, he followed her over the fields. They climbed over two fields, and when they got to the pond, Henry saw a jacket on the floor and said to Hannah.

'What's this?'

'It's arr Ada's jacket, she's in there, so is arr Emma – now go and tell your mother and father that we are going in as well, they'll have no trouble finding us!'

Shocked, Henry ran back to the inn to find his parents. Hannah was true to her word, as, within minutes, Henry heard a loud splash coming from the pond. There were no cries and no screams.

Around six in the evening, Henry Battye returned from Huddersfield, it had rained all day, and he was soaking wet. He asked his wife to remove his boots as his fingers were too cold to untie the laces. He then went upstairs to change out of his damp clothes. When he came back downstairs, his wife Anne told him that she had not seen Hannah or the children for a few hours and that she was beginning to worry about them, she had asked the neighbours after her, but nobody had seen them. A few minutes later, a very distressed 8-year-old Henry came screaming and crying into the house carrying Ada's jacket. Catching his breath, he managed to say, 'It's arr Ada's jacket. She's drowned herself and the others in the red chimney pond!' Hannah gave it to me and told me to tell you that Ada and Emma are in the pond and that she's off in there herself with the baby.

Breaking down, Ann cried,

'Pray no, please Henry, please go see.'

Henry and his son rushed from the house to the pond, it was a dark, stormy night, and they could not see anything. Henry junior showed his father the last place he had seen his sister. Knowing there was nothing they could do, the pair rushed back to the inn to inform the authorities.

Understandably, Mrs Battye was distraught when her son and husband revealed the reality of what they assumed had happened that evening. 'Aye, love,' Henry told his wife. 'I believe it's true. Best we fetch the police.'

Sergeant Hant at Shepley immediately came to the spot.

The light was poor, and it was impossible to drain the pond, so the police and Henry had to drag it. However, they managed to find some washing lines and hooks from the engine house near the dam, which they fastened to a line.

Hannah's body was the first to be discovered, followed by Ada, then Emma and the small body of baby John was brought out of the pond.

There were no signs or marks of violence on their bodies. They all just looked sullen as if they were asleep.

The bodies were taken back to the inn and laid out next to each other in the basement.

Sadly, it soon became apparent that Hannah had planned the terrible deaths of her children and had firmly made up her mind to commit this rash act. Before Hannah left her room for the last time, she had purposely laid out linen at the foot of her bed, presumably for her mother to find. The items included nightgowns, chemises, and stockings. These articles of clothing were neatly laid out, ready to receive the corpses for herself and her children.

The inquest into the deaths was held at the Junction Inn. It cannot have been easy for Mr and Mrs Battye to listen, in their own home, to the evidence about their daughter and how she had murdered her children – their grandchildren.

The Coroner, Mr Bairstow, represented the district. The jury, headed by Arthur Bennett, visited the pond and viewed the four dead bodies laid out in the inn's basement.

Both Mr and Mrs Battye put their stories forward. Henry Battye reconfirmed the conversation he had with his stepdaughter regarding telling her to leave the inn in a week.

Wallace Stringer, a road surveyor of Drop Down near New Mill, stated that he had called into the Junction Inn on that fateful day waiting to speak to Mr Battye. Whilst he waited for him to return from Huddersfield, he had played with the two youngest children in the taproom. Hannah told him what her father had said to her.

'I shall have to go.'

Wallace replied that he had heard her stepfather say that before, but she had always stayed. After that, he did not see Hannah or her children again.

Eight-year-old Henry recounted what he had seen and how Hannah had given him Ada's jacket. The coroner asked Mrs Battye about the relationship she had with her daughter. Ann explained that the relationship was strained and often stormy. She said that her daughter had all three children at her house and that Hannah was very fond of all of them. The fathers of the eldest and the youngest child contributed towards the children's keep, but the middle child, Emma's father, had died before she was born.

The inquest asked Ann what Hannah's state of mind was on the day of her death. Ann said she was in good health. She had no illness, no headaches and no pain that affected her brain. When asked if there was any madness in the family, Anne replied that her father had died of typhus fever, one of her cousins had drowned himself, and another uncle had taken poison. Ann confirmed that her daughter was not insured, but her three children were.

Once the evidence concluded, the Coroner summed up and said that the whole affair was execrable. He had heard of women murdering a child throughout his career but never three of her children. It is a terrible sad crime, and no doubt Mr and Mrs Battye had suffered immense grief over the deaths of their daughter and their three grandchildren.

The Coroner reaffirmed there was no doubt as to the cause of the family's deaths. The only doubt not established was again Hannah's state of mind on the day in question. 'There does not appear to be a scrap of evidence to show an unsound mind,' the Coroner asserted. 'It is for the jury to decide whether they return a verdict of wilful murder against Hannah in as far as the deaths of her children are concerned. Then it is up to the jury to show if there was enough evidence to determine the mother's state of mind at the time.'

The jury deliberated for over an hour then returned with a verdict of guilty of the murder of all Hannah's three children and a verdict of suicide on Hannah herself.

The coffins of Hannah and her three children were taken from the pub's basement, where they lay side by side. They were then placed on three tables outside the front door for people to pay their respects.

Six females carried Hannah, and four girls  Ada, then Emma, whilst four boys took John.

When all the coffins were in the hearse and led away, the family members followed behind first, then many others after that. Finally, the service took place, and the bodies interned in the grave.

Understandably, it was a sad and solemn affair.

R.I.P.

# 1888-1890 - The Bradford Murders. 'Alcohol The Curse of The Working Class.' (Gladstone)

Like today, in many towns and cities in industrial Britain, the people of Victorian Bradford liked to drink. There were plenty of beerhouses, gin palaces, dram shops and public houses selling alcohol to people from all walks of life. Before the 1872 Licensing Act, drinking went on from dawn to dusk.

Excessive alcohol consumption caused numerous medical and moral concerns throughout the whole country. The country's courts filled with once prosperous, hard-working people who had given way to the habits of intemperance and committed either severe or trivial crimes whilst intoxicated. In 1872, Prime Minister William Gladstone introduced the Licensing act (1872), citing alcohol as 'the curse of the working class. For the first time in England, public houses had to close and stop serving alcohol at midnight and eleven o'clock in the countryside (to ensure men were home by midnight).

Women were just as bad who frequented gin palaces in most towns. Some women deviated from the norm, and many were undoubtedly not angels as some men expected in many Victorian households. Often women would take their husband's Sunday best clothes to the pawnbroker on Monday morning, then on a Saturday when the husband got paid, the suit would come out of the pledge and returned them the following Monday.

Excessive bouts of alcohol consumption sadly fuel the following two terrible cases of murder in Victorian Bradford.

* * *

# CHAPTER 7

## 1888. Darley Street Bradford – The Murder of Esther Neale.

*Darley Street, Bradford. Author's collection.*

Francis Willian Neale, a native of Norfolk, was, for many years, employed in a hosiery shop at Leeds and afterwards as an assistant for Messrs. J Holmes & Co. He married his wife Esther in 1869, and together they ran a successful draper's shop at 14 Darley Street Bradford, initially established by Mrs Neale's mother, Mrs Smith, who had retired to Scarborough.

Before her marriage, people thought of Mrs Neale as a well-conducted young lady who always had a smile for everyone. Her marriage, it seems, was a disastrous turning point in her life. The couple was happy for most of their marriage, but the last six years were catastrophic due to Mrs Neale's constant insobriety. In drink, which was often, she was a very quarrelsome woman, and the couple's many drunken brawls often disturbed the peace of Grosvenor Street, Belle Vue, Manningham, Bradford where they lived.

Even at their workplace, the Neale's didn't hide their contempt for each other, and they would argue and bicker even with a shop full of customers. A police officer stationed opposite the couple's shop on Darley Street had to interfere to prevent them from injuring each other when he heard cries of murder coming from the shop. When the officer investigated what was happening, he found that Mrs Neale was the one striking out. Mr Neale had not laid a hand on his wife.

In the afternoon of Friday, June 8th, 1888, Mrs Neale was working in the shop and was in her usual argumentative mood after drinking most of the day. By mid-afternoon, she had sobered up a little, but by teatime, she had already had two blazing rows with her husband. Finally, at seven in the evening, closing time. The shop assistant, Miss Bentley, left the premises leaving Mrs Neale in the shop with her twelve-year-old son William, and John Black, a concrete layer who lived at Carlisle Terrace, Manningham, Bradford, who had called into the shop to see Mr Neale. As Mr Neale was not there, Mrs Neale sent her son home and persuaded Mr Black to stay with her until she locked the shop up, and then he could accompany her home. Mrs Neale went upstairs to fetch her bonnet, and Mr Black waited for her downstairs. A short time later, Mrs Neale shouted for Mr Black to go upstairs. When he did so, he was shocked to find Mrs Neale naked except for her stockings and boots.

Soon after, Mr Neale appeared and caught the couple together. In anger, he yelled, 'I have caught you in the act!' There was a sweeping brush nearby with a red handle; he picked it up and tried to strike Black with it. Black managed to run downstairs and escape into the street. Neale went back inside to confront his wife, dressed in a chemise and a red flannel vest. A scuffle between the couple and Mrs Neale had blood on her face and over one of her eyes. Her husband bathed her face with a cloth and told her to get herself washed and dressed and go home. Mr Neale then left his wife and went for a drink at the White Lion pub. He then went back to the shop; his wife was still there but had fallen onto the floor. She was dead, her face distorted with blood oozing from her mouth as if she had had a fit. Mr Neale covered her in a coat and left the shop.

Mr Neale then went to the Airedale Pub in Otley Road, where he saw Mr Cockroft, Mrs Neale's cousin. Neale told this cousin that he had caught his wife with another man, but he hadn't done anything to her but said, 'Etty is laid dead in the shop.' Cockroft asked if he had sent for a doctor, and Neale said he hadn't. So the men went together back to the shop where Cockroft later described the scene: 'She was lying on the floor of an upper back room, clad only in a chemise and a red vest. The room was in disarray. There were two broken windows and glass on the floor, her head resting on a coat loosely thrown over the dead woman. Some of her clothing had been thrown out of the window and was lying in the street. Her body was still warm, so she can't have been dead long.' It all looked suspicious to me.

Police arrived on the scene, but there was little they could do. Finally, superintendent Laycock sent a cab for police surgeon Mr Lodge, who could do nothing except to pronounce Mrs Neale dead on his arrival. He ordered the removal of her body to the cemetery so that a post-mortem could take place. On examination, the doctor found several bruises on the body, which appeared to have been caused by kicks or blows. There was also a wound at the back of the head and large bruises on her back and thighs. At that time, it was unclear as to whether this was the cause of death. In the meantime, Mr Neale was arrested and taken into custody for the murder of his wife.

The post-mortem revealed that Mrs Neale had suffered extreme violence. Five of her ribs were broken, and blows inflicted to the lower part of her body.

An inquest was held at Bradford Town Hall on the Monday following the murder. The Coroner, Mr JG Hutchinson, opened the enquiry. Miss Bentley, the shop assistant, was the first witness. She retold her story and added that the couple had a row over who would make the evening tea. This lack of preparation was a recurring problem as Mrs Neale had not made a meal in quite a few weeks and was a constant source of argument. Mr Neale also complained that his wife had been staying out on a night, but she refused to say where she had been or who she was with. Mrs Neale had been drinking for many weeks and was not often sober; the day of the murder, she had been drinking most of the day and was quite drunk in the afternoon.

Mr Neale was not pleased and, at one point, told his wife to go upstairs and wash her face as she looked dirty. She laughed at her husband and replied, 'No, I shan't, I'm as clean as you are.' Mr Neale responded, 'Do as you like,' and walked out of the shop.

Mrs Neale had complained of a headache all day. She had a large lump behind her ear and went entirely white at one point, and had to sit on a stool behind the register. However, Mrs Neale cheered up a little when Mr Black entered the store. Miss Bentley confirmed that the Neale's had constant arguments for the last two months, and she had seen Mr Neale strike his wife on more than one occasion. Miss Bentley finished her shift. She did not see Mrs Neale again.

William Neale, the couple's son, gave evidence and said that he saw his father strike his mother quite a few times, especially over the last two months. William said his father usually struck her on the back, but he had often been worse for a drink in the previous two weeks and had hit his mother more frequently. The boy added that his mother was violent when she was drinking, but William had never seen her strike his father. He said his mother had not been coming home in an evening because his father hit her. Although a couple of months earlier, his mother had an accident at home when she was drunk and started throwing chairs around the house, she was so drunk she fell down the cellar steps and had been taken to the infirmary.

John Black recounted that he was a friend of Mr Neale's as they had done business before, and he had gone to the shop to talk to him. 'I often called into the shop but in a friendly way—nothing else. Mrs Black asked me to stay and help her close the shop, so I agreed. Mrs Neale then went upstairs for her bonnet, coat and keys and some other bits and bats. She didn't come down, so I shouted up to her. She asked me to go upstairs, hollering to me, 'come up, I want you.' I went upstairs and found her sitting on a box at the back of the shop; she was naked except for her stockings and boots. I was shocked and said, 'Good heavens, Mrs Neale, what are you doing?' She replied, 'Come over here and sit down beside me. I am going to stay here tonight.' She asked me again to come to her, I went to the end of the box and put my hand on her shoulder, and I asked her to get dressed. At that same moment, her husband, Mr Neale, came to the top of the steps. He was smoking a clay pipe. On seeing his wife in a state of undress with another man, he was outraged and screamed at me, 'I've caught you, you bastard.' He continued swearing at me, calling me a villain, a coward, and many other names. He then threatened to smash me and kill me, and he reached for the broomstick and attempted to strike me with it. I grabbed the broom and told him not to strike and that I would explain the full circumstances tomorrow, but they were not what he assumed. I then tried to leave, and Neale chased after me.

When I left Mrs Neale, there were no broken windows, and the furniture was not in disarray. Mrs Neale continued to sit in the same position on the ottoman box. She was uninjured.'

Thomas Cartwright, the landlord of The White Lion Vaults, Kirkgate, Bradford, said the accused came into his pub around 9.40 pm on the night of the murder. He was without a hat and seemed excited. He had a bruise on his forehead and asked if he could borrow a hat, as he had lost his witnessing a fight on Darley Street opposite his shop involving two young men. I asked him what type of men they were. He said they looked like respectable young men, but he didn't know who they were, and he added that one of the men got carted off to the infirmary. Mr Neale was served with two pence worth of rum and a cigar. He had left by the back door, and Cartwright hadn't seen him again.

John Cockroft, the landlord of the Airedale Inn, Bradford and cousin of Mrs Neale, said, 'I last saw Mrs Neale at a room above her shop on Friday the day she died. The room was unorganised with dirty pots and pans. Her husband was there, and they were quarrelling. Mrs Neale wanted to wash and clean the room, but her husband insisted that she washed and went to serve in the shop. They were both in a high temper, and I asked them to calm down, and I left. I next saw Mr Neale at around 10.40 in the commercial room at the Airedale Inn. Neale said:

'I believe Etty is dead.'

I asked him for what reason he thought she was dead. 'I cannot move her.'

I asked him if he had called a doctor, and to my dismay, he said he hadn't. So I was furious and asked him why he'd come here first and not go for a doctor.

'Will you come with me?' he pleaded.

No, I said, you get a doctor, and I will follow.

We both set off towards the shop on Darley Street; on the way, we met PCs Gibson and Parsons, who went with the men to the shop. Esther Neale's body was covered in a blanket on the upper floor. Mr Cockroft was sickened as he recognised his cousin and realised she was dead. He held up her hand, and it was stone cold. Mr Neale returned twenty minutes later when he was arrested for the murder of his wife and taken into custody.

'I have not touched her,' he sobbed.

On his way to the Town Hall, he continued preaching his innocence. Finally, turning to me, he said, 'Cousin, I never touched her, I promise.'

I wasn't happy and responded, "That remains to be seen. Let's see what the jury says about that". Inconsolable, Neale burst into tears.

Whilst in the police cells, the prisoner said to the police officer in charge. 'This is a bad job; I wish I could see an end to it. There is nobody that can say I did it because I didn't. I did kick her. I admit that, but that would not kill a woman in her state.'

Police surgeon Samuel Lodge, Wakefield Road, gave evidence as to the results of his post-mortem. He reported that the abdomen of Esther Neale was soft, warm, and swollen; he could not smell drink on her body. Blood flowed from a small cut on her scalp, her pupils dilated but clear. There were many bruises on her arms. Her right hip was very swollen and showed signs of trauma and violence. On opening her abdomen, it was filled with fresh blood arising from the perforation of the left kidney. Her liver, kidneys, and bladder, along with her lungs, were all perfectly healthy. However, every rib below her chest was fractured. The cause of her death was a rupture of the lungs and significant internal bleeding. The surgeon concluded that death would have been almost immediate.

One of the jurors asked Doctor Lodge a question, 'If Mrs Neale had died of a fit, would there have been signs of this in the examination?'

Doctor Lodge confirmed that it would have shown up, but he established a fit was not the cause of death.

This evidence closed the enquiry, and the Coroner addressed the jury, bringing to their attention the law on homicide which was that murder was not rendered justifiable or excusable by provocation. Still, if stimulation was given to such an extent to excite the man significantly, then manslaughter should be the verdict. He also pointed out that if a man caught his wife in the act of adultery and killed a man on the spot, then manslaughter would be the crime.

The jury retired. After an absence of five minutes, they returned with a verdict of manslaughter. Neale was brought before the Coroner and committed for trial at the next Leeds Assizes. Neale looked in a sorry state, pale and ill. His defence team asked for bail. The Coroner said he would give the matter his consideration the following day.

It was 4th August before Neale came to trial at Leeds Assizes. Mr BR Stansfield and Mr Whittaker Thompson appeared for the prosecution, and Mr Waugh acted for the defence. Once the evidence was heard, Mr Waugh put his case to the jury, saying in mitigation this was the first occasion that the prisoner had used violence to his wife (despite her son William and the shop assistant stating otherwise at a previous hearing). Mr Neale had to put up with the often violent, drunken unhappy woman for the last six eight years. In that time, he had been provoked into striking his wife, and finding her in a drunken state, naked with another man was more than he or many a man could take, and the poor man had tried his best to bring his wife back to habits of virtue, to no avail. The lawyer added that he, a man of law, would most probably have acted the same way if faced with similar circumstances. However, Neale did what he did under intense excitement and with incredible frustration. Under the circumstances, he asked His Lordship to deal leniently with the prisoner who had already been in custody for two months.

At this point, Mr Waugh advised the prisoner to withdraw his original plea and changed his plea to guilty.

On summing up, His Lordship addressed the prisoner and said that upon reading the deposition. He concluded that Neale, unfortunately, had a wife who was of intemperate habits. Yet to the prisoner's knowledge, she had not been unfaithful. However, when he found his wife with another man, he did what any other man would do. He kicked the man down the stairs.

Regarding the wife, the prisoner was obviously in a frenzy of rage and temper. He knocked her down and kicked her, causing her death. He was undoubtedly guilty of manslaughter. However, there are differing degrees of this crime. As the prisoner had already been in gaol for two months, and bearing in mind the circumstances of the crime, he could not justify giving the prisoner more than a sentence of one day's imprisonment. Taking all points into account, he ordered the prisoner to be released.

As the prisoner left the court, there was a round of applause, which the judge stopped immediately.

R.I.P Esther Neale. A troubled and unhappy lady.

# CHAPTER 8

# 1890. Murder & Suicide – Wilsden Bradford – Ezekiel Sutcliffe.

*Shay Gate, Wilsden. Credit David Beck.*

In the early hours of Saturday 23rd August 1890, the peaceful village of Wilsden near Bradford was ablaze with rumours of murder and suicide. By noon, these rumours were found to be well-founded and later confirmed. Ezekiel Sutcliffe, his wife Jane, and their children lived at 22 Shay Gate, Wilsden. The house was one in a row of cottages owned by Mrs Toothill, which she rented to tenants at two shillings a week. Villagers soon testified that Ezekiel had murdered his wife and then committed suicide.

They quickly pointed out that Mr Sutcliffe had suffered a long time with odd, strange behaviour. One man who had known the family for a long time said, 'Tek my word for it, he's wrong in his head, and I believe that's been the case o' t trouble.'

Jane Sutcliffe was forty-four and three years older than her husband. A native of Haworth, her neighbours, described her as a good mother and a hard worker. The couple had six children; the eldest two boys worked away from home. Mrs Sutcliffe took pride in her children, who were always clean and tidy. She did not mingle with the neighbours too much. Although always polite, she kept herself to herself. She was known to nag at her husband often but most likely with good cause.

Mr and Mrs Sutcliffe slept in a box or 'shut up bed' on the house's ground floor. Their four children slept upstairs in a room divided by a roughly made wood partition. On the night of the murder, the children were all in bed by eleven-thirty. They were sick of the constant bickering of their parents and left them to it. Their father was the loudest, and arguments were a regular occurrence. The children stayed awake for a short time then fell asleep.

Jane went to bed first and was in a deep sleep when the deed occurred. It is most probable that Mr Sutcliffe did not go to bed but instead drunk himself into a frenzy. It seems that Mr Sutcliffe did not lie by his wife's side that night, but instead, he knelt and strangled his wife quickly and silently. None of the children heard anything.

About two-thirty, in the morning James Sutcliffe, aged twelve, was awoken by his young sister asking him to fetch her a glass of water. He went downstairs and saw his mother lying in her bed; she was noticeably quiet with her hands laid across her breast. His father's jacket and waistcoat lay at the foot of the bed. James put his ear close to her mouth to see if she was asleep or dead. He lit a match and tried to speak to her. At that time, he heard a shuffling noise in the cellar. Thinking it was his father's footsteps, James went back upstairs carrying the glass of water with trepidation.

There is little doubt that the father would have heard his son get out of bed, so he hid in the cellar after which, he put on his coat, vest and cap and hastily made his way to the mill at Birks Head. Running across the fields, he would have to climb the wire fencing to get in. The dam was only four feet deep. Here he ended his life.

Robert Hornby found him in the pond, with Sutcliffe's head embedded in the mud at the bottom of the dam, his feet sticking out of the water.

*The X in the window marks - where the happened*

The motive for the murder was jealousy fuelled by alcohol. Mr Sutcliffe had for some time suspected that his wife was being unfaithful and was having an affair. This suspicion was utterly unfounded. Through years of drinking, Sutcliffe had become paranoid and quite demented. The family had moved to Wilsden in the winter of 1889. Before that, they lived in

Egypt near Thornton, Bradford. They were known locally as 'The Walls of Jericho' because of the number of quarries in the area. Ezekiel worked for eight years at Bell Dean quarries, where he was well respected and known as a hard-working, industrious man. When he moved to Wilsden, he gave way to drink and soon, his anger and paranoia got out of control. He would often watch his house for a man he knew from Thornton, who he thought kept visiting his wife.

*The Dam where they found the body. (X) marks the spot.*

The room where they found the body was untidy, but this was not a poor house. Friday had been cleaning day, although it was evident that Mrs Sutcliffe must have been distracted that Friday as she had not cleaned the house. There were photographs on the wall, brass candlesticks on the fireplace. The floor was flagged and uncarpeted. There was a rocking chair in the corner of the room with a well-worn sheepskin rug thrown over the back of it. A plain side table with some unwashed cups and saucers on it, there were more dirty pots and pans on the dresser. A washing line was suspended across the room with various pieces of laundry on it, with another pile on a chair all neatly folded and mended.

From the foot of the put-up bed facing the fireplace, upon the left-hand side of the bed looking from the foot, lay the ghostly white body of Mrs Sutcliffe covered in a blanket. Her eyes were deeply sunken. Her cheeks hollow, her lips thin. Her hands were white and bony. On the left side of her neck were the imprints of her murderer's fingers. The marks were black and deeply embedded as if he had forced his nails deep into her flesh.

When brought out of the dam, Ezekiel Sutcliffe's body was laid on his back. He had a fierce expression on his face, which was covered in thick clay type mud. His thick dark hair and whiskers were all matted.

Both bodies were interned together at Horton cemetery. Husband and wife – murdered and murderer.

The inquest held at the Brown Cow Inn, Ling Bob, before deputy Coroner Mr TE Hill. Sutcliffe's eldest son John Gibson Sutcliffe said that he last saw his parents alive on Monday morning when he left home. His father was for some reason jealous of his mother and had convinced himself that she was having an affair.

James then told the story of how he went downstairs to get his sister a glass of water. He added that when he returned upstairs and laid on the floor looking downstairs from a crack in the floorboards. James daren't move but stayed there until he was sick with worry, then he went back to bed. He did not sleep well and woke for work at the usual time of six. Although, he did not go to work. 'I crept downstairs with my sister convinced that my mother was dead, although we did not go into the room where she slept as we were too frightened. My sister ran to tell our neighbour Mrs Lee, and I ran to tell our landlady, Mrs Toothill. Mrs Toothill came then told us 'your mother is dead'.'

Mr Richard Alexander Eden, a surgeon practising at Wilsden, performed the post-mortem on Jane Sutcliffe on Sunday. His report concluded that she was a well-nourished middle-aged woman and that on the left side of her neck about an inch in diameter with some deep scratches. There were also ruptured blood vessels in her scalp. Death, he concluded, was caused by strangulation.

Robert Hornby, a weaver from Wilsden, said that he found Ezekiel Sutcliffe's body in the mill dam at Birks Head on Saturday night. He ran for assistance. There was no evidence to show how he got into the dam.

The deputy Coroner summed up that Mrs Sutcliffe had died from strangulation, murdered by her husband, and afterwards, he had committed suicide whilst of unsound mind.

* * *

# CHAPTER 9

# 1890. Bedale. The Shocking Murder of Sergeant Weedy.

© *Yorkshire Evening Post 1890.*

Early on Saturday morning, September 19th, 1890, Mr and Mrs Kettlewell took their usual journey to Richmond Market from their home in Exley, followed by Mr Fred Hollands, huntsman from the Bedale Hunt. As they approached the village of Leeming, they were alarmed to find the well-known police sergeant, James Weedy, lying dead in a pool of blood. The officer's lamp and stick were at his side and his cloak strewn close by on a grass verge.

Sergeant Weedy and a man named Robert Kitching lived a few doors away from each other in the semi-rural village of Leeming. It was common knowledge that Kitching and the police officer had an intense dislike of each other for many years, and their personalities often clashed. James Weedy was an exemplary police officer who had been in the force for twenty years. Married with twelve children, he was well-liked, and people described him as a diligent, intelligent, and brave officer. The latter, in his work, feared nothing or nobody, especially when dealing with poachers. He was a dedicated police sergeant who didn't suffer fools gladly. Robert Kitching was at the top of Weedy's list of 'undesirable scalawags.'

Kitching, a market gardener and seedsman, had returned to his native town of Leeming after declaring bankruptcy in Boroughbridge five years earlier, where he had suffered an accident when a gun exploded, taking off his left hand. This incident caused him to wear a hook in his sleeve – an implement which, in drink, reports say he gouged men's faces and even ripped their eyes out. Throughout the community, people feared Kitching, who had been before the magistrates many times for severe assaults. The week before the murder, he appeared before the magistrates for being drunk and disorderly. None of his neighbours had a good word to say for him and considered him a dangerous character.

On the night of the murder, Kitching had been drinking all afternoon and evening in the Leeming Bar Hotel (now the Corner House Hotel), leaving his horse and cart outside, unlit, on the busy Great North Road. He soon became raucous, noisy, and troublesome and started a fight with his neighbour Mr Dale, screwing off his hook, ready to hit him. As the night drew in, Weedy was doing his usual rounds and asked Kitching to go outside and move his horse and cart. At first, Kitching refused. Weedy responded, 'Go home, I don't want any nonsense. Suppose you don't do as I say. In that case, I will have to report you!' after a bit of coaxing by others, Kitching left, swearing oaths and chuntering his usual bad-tempered threats against the policeman. The latter, six months earlier, had reported him for using this same cart as an unlicensed taxi. On his way out, customers heard him shout. 'I will do him. I will. I will shoot him. I'll blow his bloody brains out.'

Mr Frank Lewis, the pub landlord, took no notice. He had heard Kitching make similar claims many times before – this bothersome customer had been a constant source of trouble all day, and he was glad to see the back of him. Kitching left the pub ten minutes past ten, followed three-quarters of an hour later by Sergeant Weedy. Kitching was watching out for him from his window and seeing him. He ran outside, shouting obscenities at the officer. At this, Weedy stopped and went through Kitching's gate. A drunken Kitching told the officer not to trespass any further into his garden. If he did, then he would shoot him. Unperturbed, Weedy took no notice of the drunken man's threats and took a step closer. Enraged, Kitching lunged forward, placed the gun close to the officer's neck, and pulled the trigger. Weedy died instantly.

After the fatal deed, Kitching placed the unspent cartridges on the kitchen table. He then realised that his wife and children were not in the house. Assuming they were at his father-in-law Edmund Caygill's house, he went to find them. Still agitated, Kitching admitted to Caygill that he had killed Weedy. Kitching and his father-in-law went to the nearby beck, and Kitching threw the gun into the water, shouting, 'there, I'm done with that.' Both men then went back to the crime scene and moved the dead man's body to the side of the road where someone would see it.

Someone must have heard gunshots throughout the neighbourhood, yet nobody saw anything or looked out of their windows as the police officer lay dead on the grass opposite Kitching's gate. He lay undiscovered the whole night, exposed to the elements and the drenching rain.

The Kettlewell's discovered the body at 5.30 in the morning; they informed the police, who removed Weedy to the local joiner's workshop. The medical officer confirmed that the gunshot had penetrated the top part of the deceased's waistcoat, took an upward direction from the base of the neck, and ricocheted into the lower brain, which killed him.

Around the village, Kitching's long-suffering wife Jane and their four children received a degree of sympathy. Jane had a miserable life with him, and the house they lived in was ramshackle with an overgrown garden with an old plum tree in the middle. On the night of the shooting, her husband returned from his mammoth drinking session in a foul and thunderous rage, yelling at the top of his voice that he wanted to shoot 'that bastard Weedy'. Jane lived in fear of her husband, and she tried her utmost to calm him down, to no avail. He shoved her aside, telling her he would shoot her as well if she didn't get out of his way. Terrified, she waited until her husband left the house, then she took her four-month-old baby and fled to her neighbour, Mrs Dale's house, who lived next door but then collected her other three children and took shelter there. Not long after she got the children settled into bed, she heard a gunshot. The time was eleven o'clock. Nobody dared move.

Still looking for his wife, Kitching banged on his neighbour's doors to see if they had seen his wife and children – they all said no. Kitching then went to bed. The following morning, he got up as usual and prepared his cart for the market. His father-in-law had tried to persuade him not to go, but Kitching was insistent that he had a barrel full of plums he didn't want to spoil and a pig he tried to shift. He wasn't there long before Inspector Holmes, and Superintendent Nicholson apprehended him working on his stall at Richmond Market and charged him with murder. Kitching appeared shocked, shouting. 'What me? They can't blame me!' After a struggle, the police took Kitching into custody to await trial at the Bedale Petty Sessions.

Evidence showed that Weedy's death was instantaneous. Kitching did what witnesses claimed he said he would do before he left the pub. 'I will blow that bastard's brains out.' A threat he'd often said when drunk, but nobody believed he would carry it out.

The public sympathised with Mrs Weedy. Overnight she'd lost her husband and her livelihood. With twelve children, the youngest only five months to support, it overwhelmed the poor lady. In response to her plight, the public set up a fund, donations flooded in with over four hundred pounds collected.

James Weedy's funeral took place at Leeming village church, attended by 1200 people, including a significant police presence from all divisions; he was well respected. The sergeant's remains were placed in a polished pine coffin, laid with wreaths and crosses from several of the deceased's sympathisers from all over the district—a procession headed by the 1st

Volunteer Battalion Yorkshire Regiment played the Dead March. On arriving at the churchyard, the choir sang 'My God, my father, whilst I stray'. Every space in the church was full, and the Rev W Dennison read the funeral service. The choir finished with the hymn 'On the resurrection morning'.

Captain Carter presided over the first inquest into the police officer's death at the Assembly Rooms at Bedale Petty Sessions on 30th September 1890. The prisoner travelled to the inquest on a third-class train carriage. Herds of people crammed the railway platforms along the way, hoping for a glimpse of the man who murdered a village policeman. As soon as the doors opened, hundreds of people scrambled inside the rooms, whilst hundreds more assembled outside. As Kitching entered the Assembly Rooms, he looked anxious and sad and tried his best to ignore the derogatory remarks aimed at him.

The prosecution opened the case declaring that all evidence proved that the fatal shot could not have happened by accident and that the shooting was intentional. Various witnesses put forward evidence, including neighbour Catherine Metcalfe, wife of labourer William. Catherine said she had a clear memory of the night of the murder. She and her husband had gone to bed around ten. After being in bed some time, Mrs Kitching heard rumbling sounds outside, and shortly after, a voice she thought was Robert Kitching's saying something, but she wasn't quite sure what except hearing the word bastard, which was typical of him. She then listened to the clack of the gate. The following day, she saw a man lying in the green opposite her window. She discerned it was a policeman by his belt.

The inquest lasted six hours when the jury decided that Kitching should stand trial at the York Assizes. The worried prisoner returned to custody at Northallerton Gaol.

Whilst on remand, Kitching sent for his wife to go over the directions for his defence. In gaol and without alcohol, Kitching soon realised the seriousness of his rash actions. As he realised the gravity of what he'd done, his health suffered, and he was taken to the prison hospital. Kitching told his wife and other visitors that he did not realise that he was facing the possibility of death and that he expected to get five years of penal servitude. His health deteriorated, and he suffered greatly with regret and remorse. His condition became so severe that the authorities thought he would not be fit enough to plead his case at his trial scheduled for December.

There was a big crush for seats when the court opened its door for the trial at Yorkshire Assizes on December 9th. Every seat in the court was taken, and a large crowd gathered outside. Every eye in the court turned in the direction of the dock when the accused took the stand. The prisoner looked worn and anxious. All the hard-headed bravado Kitching was well known for had disappeared.

Mr Luck and Mrs Meek conducted the prosecution under the instruction of the solicitor to the treasurer. Mr Waddy QC, MP, was for the defence. The charge of the wilful murder of James Weedy on 19th September 1890 was read out to the prisoner who, when asked how he pleaded, the prisoner replied, 'not guilty'. Kitching was then allowed to take his seat.

At first, Weedy claimed the shooting was an accident. Then he claimed that Weedy had struck the first blow with a stick. But his father-in-law, Edmund Caygill, with whom he had spent the chaotic hours between the shooting and his arrest on the market, was unable – or unwilling — to corroborate either story.

Witness Robert Lambert said he and Kitching were drinking together in the Leeming Bar Hotel from 3 pm till closing time. By the end of the evening, Kitching was in a foul mood and had threatened a few customers, including himself.

Frank Lewis, the pub landlord, remembered Sergeant Weedy popping his head around the pub door, saying, 'Kitching, I want you to get yourself and that horse and cart home, or I will have to report you!' To which Kitching expelled many obscenities followed with 'I will go home when I'm ready.'

John Kettlewell gave evidence; he was a blacksmith and greengrocer who had discovered Weedy's body on his way to the market. Joiner, George Hudson, declared he had the sergeant's body in his coach house and said that he found a hole near the collar of the tunic he was wearing on examining the body. Surgeon, Thomas Horsfall, examined Weedy's body. The policeman's head and his right arm were turned to the right.

He found a large hole near the tunic's shoulder on the left-hand side and a gaping lacerated hole in his neck, obviously from a gunshot, indicating that the gun was fired at a short distance.

No witnesses were called in Kitching's defence, but it soon became apparent that Weedy and Kitching had a deep-rooted hatred for each other. Such malice existed between them that Weedy reported his enemy to the Inland Revenue several times. At the time of the murder, a Revenue Officer, Mr Joseph Kirby from Bedale, asked Weedy to keep surveillance on the prisoner as he did not have a licence for the trap he was using.

The learned judge commenced his summing up. Finally, he directed the jury to consider the questions. On the night of the tragedy, how could they account for the actions of the prisoner's wife? There could only be two possibilities. Either the prisoner had threatened 'to do' his wife and children, so she had made a hasty retreat to her neighbour's house. Or she had left as he avowed vengeance against the policeman, as he had threatened he would earlier in the evening? Why would a wife leave her home unless she was in danger? Furthermore, if, as the prisoner suggested, the shooting was accidental, then why did he go outside with a gun in his hand, and why did he move the body and not call for help?

Suppose the prisoner discharged the gun in a struggle and overpowered. Then he would be guilty of manslaughter. Still, if they concluded that he went to the gate armed with a gun to carry out the deed that he threatened earlier in the evening – then that would be murder.

The jury retired for half an hour, and Kitching was put back in the dock where he awaited the verdict.

'Gentleman of the jury, are you agreed upon your verdict? Do you find the prisoner Robert Kitching guilty or not guilty?'

'Guilty' – although they added a recommendation for mercy.

The judge asked the prisoner if he had anything to say about why the sentence should not be passed. In an inaudible voice, Kitching hung his head and answered 'no'.

There was perfect stillness around the courtroom as Judge Lawrence assumed the black cap and passed the death sentence.

Kitching jumped to his feet and, in a rambling, incoherent stream of consciousness, said, 'I did wrong that night, I shouldn't have taken the gun outside, but Weedy would not be dead if he hadn't walked through the gate. It was an accident. Weedy rushed at me and struck me with his stick, and accidentally the gun went off. Here I am sentenced to death, but I'm not guilty of wilful murder. I'm a respectable man. I've been married for ten years, and I've four children. If people feared me, then they wouldn't patronise my goods at the market. I was drunk. It was the drink. Let the Lord have mercy on you – to incline in your hearts to prevent this. Lord, help me.' The prisoner broke down, and he had to be helped to his seat. A warder asked if he wanted to say anything else, he did, 'Please, give me another chance, the evidence is not correct – it was an accident!'

The judge donned the black cap and was surprisingly abrupt. He dismissed the prisoner's statement. He said, 'The sentence is one which the law compels me to pass upon you. That sentence is that you be taken from hence to the place of execution. From there, you will be hanged by the neck until you are dead. Afterwards, your body is to be buried within the prison grounds in which you were last confined. In line with the jury's wishes, I will forward to the proper quarter the recommendation to mercy, but I can hold out no hope that that will lead to any commutation of your sentence.' May God, in His infinite wisdom, have mercy on your soul.

Kitching received the sentence with a blanched face, but he uttered no sound as he walked from the dock.

The Home Secretary dismissed all pleas for clemency, and as the day of justice fast approached, the condemned man bitterly blamed his father-in-law for not fabricating an alibi for him.

The execution took place on 30th December 1890. Robert Kitching's last hours were agonising. He spent a restless night not able to sleep or eat. He spent his last hour in prayer, and terrible unrest came upon him.  It was four in the morning before the warders persuaded him to lie down on his pallet, but he couldn't sleep at all. He said his final prayers in the chapel before being taken to the condemned cell adjoining the scaffold erected in the old part of the prison. Nerves took over, and the prisoner became agitated, almost fainting.

The Governor, Sheriff and Medical Officer visited the cell with the hangman, James Billington. Upon the Governor gently touching the condemned man on the shoulder, Kitching arose from his knees and, without speaking, submitted to the pinioning process. He said nothing further but trembled violently.

When Kitching was put into position on the trap and his legs pinioned deftly by Billington, who then placed the rope around his neck, and the noose adjusted, the white handkerchief put over his face. Kitching sobbed uncontrollably and had to be supported by the wardens. He fainted and staggered. Billington drew back the lever – the trap flew down with his weight, and he met his maker. Death was instantaneous.

Robert Kitching was buried in the prison grounds, like many others before him. Before his death, Kitching admitted that he shot Sergeant Weedy. It was no accident.

The following April, widow Jane Kitching applied for poor relief for her and her four children. Sympathisers raised the sum of £112 for her and her family. Jane told the panel she had to leave her house and move in with her father. The board refused her application, declaring that the widow had a roof over her head and was not destitute. Therefore they were not in a position to assist her. However, an anonymous donor came forward with £100 to be paid to Mrs Kitching by weekly instalments of ten shillings.

R.I.P Sergeant James Weedy – fatally shot in the line of duty.

# CHAPTER 10

## 1900 – Star Fold Beeston Leeds - The Strange Murder of Mary Ann Blewitt.

*Star fold, Beeston Hill- Authors own collection.*

At Star Fold Beeston Hill, June 1900. Mary Ann Blewitt, a thirty-two-year-old married woman, was found dead at her home under suspicious circumstances. Mary was found sitting in a rocking chair, her legs outstretched and her throat cut from ear to ear.

Mary Ann originated from Morley but had moved to Beeston with her husband Charles Oliver Blewitt four years earlier. Hard-working Mary worked at a local tannery; neighbours saw her last the previous evening whitening her doorstep. The following day the house is locked, and all the curtains closed. It seems the couple had gone away, which the neighbours put down to Mr Blewitt being unemployed for the last 6-8 weeks; they assumed they had gone to look for him some work.

Uneasiness prevailed among the neighbours. They sensed something wrong, but none were sure what. The Blewitt's, like everyone else, had their quarrels, but nothing untoward. The Blewitt family were well known in Morley. Mary Ann Jackson lived with her parents in New Street before marrying her husband. Her parents had since died. Charles grandfather, eighty-year-old Mr Henry Blewitt, lived at 31 Wesley Street. He strenuously defended his grandson Charlie, saying 'he was a good lad and would hurt nobody, especially his wife.' Whilst in Morley, Blewitt had worked as a currier, then later a coal miner. Unfortunately, he didn't seem to be able to keep a job for very long.

The house at Star Fold was a squalid two-bedroom cottage owned by Mr Thomas Armitage, who lived at Town Street. When he collected the rent, he was concerned to see the house quiet and the curtains closed, not happy he returned the following day. A neighbour came out and said, 'there's nobody at home – not since Friday night.' Soon after, Mr Blewitt's mother, Mrs Bunney and her husband James called at the house demanding entry, saying something in the place belonged to them and needed to get it out now. Did Mr Armitage have a key? They also noted that the young couple had gone away in a hurry on business, although they knew where they were. The Blewitt's hadn't given the parents time to get their possessions out before they left. The landlord wasn't happy the couple owed rent, and he would not open the house until they paid the outstanding rent of 5s 6d. They all met the following morning.

The next day, the Bunny's handed over the rent money, the landlord struggled to find the right key out his bunch, with no success he smashed the door down; 'Now you can go inside.' The stepfather went into the kitchen, the mother and landlord stayed outside. One neighbour, Mrs Rudd, hearing a commotion, came out and went into Blewitt's house. The stepfather shouted, 'She's here all right' as he walked into the front room and saw his daughter-in-law sitting in a chair. Her legs stretch out, and she had a shawl over her head. Mrs Rudd removed the shawl and shrieked.

Mrs Blewitt was dead with a gaping gash across her throat. Mr Armitage said, 'Well, she's dead all right. It looks like he's killed her and fled.' Then, without looking at anything else, he went to find a police officer.

PC Freeman arrived on the scene. He went into the living room and saw the supper plates on the table – splattered with the victim's blood. The furniture not disarranged, and there were no signs that a struggle had taken place. PC Freeman rushed upstairs, half-expecting to find the murderer hiding there. The house was empty. The policeman found strange objects downstairs, such as three carving knives, two hatchets, a razor and a shoemaker's knife. This knife had a dark stain on it.

An inquest into the murder took place at 2.30 the same afternoon of discovering the body at The Railway Hotel Beeston. The pub is known locally as 'The Jerry'. The victim's brother George Jackson, a fettler who lived at Valley Road Morley, identified the victim, saying that his sister was happily married as far as he knew. Dr Head, the city surgeon, recorded that Mary had a deep laceration to her throat, severing her windpipe and blood vessels. There was a deep wound on her left wrist, cutting through the tendons. The little finger of her right hand had a cut, as was her thumb, indicating that the injury to her throat was a homicide and not a suicide. The Coroner, Mr Malcolm, adjourned the inquest given the ongoing police investigations. He permitted Mary's funeral to take place the following day.

Evidence showed that Charles Blewitt visited the local barber around 8.30 on the night of the murder. He had his hair cut and his distinguishable moustache shaved. Major Terry, Chief Constable of Leeds, issued a wanted poster for the missing man. Police produced a sketch from a photograph taken nine years earlier, showing Blewitt's distinctive moustache.

Charles Blewitt was thirty-two to thirty-five years old, fair hair, 5ft 6 inches tall, stout build, clean-shaven. A native of Copper House Cornwall, he lived in America for eleven years, where he had a nasty bang on his head, which changed his personality. His mother claimed, 'I've seen him sit in an armchair and for some minutes he would ramble like a madman, and when he came to his senses, he was peculiar, he wasn't like that before.' The poster said Blewitt was wanted for the wilful murder of his wife by cutting her throat on 8th June 1900.

Mary's funeral was a quiet affair. The procession left the house shortly after 3 pm and comprised a hearse and two cabs occupied by the victim's relatives and six of her workmates. The coffin was Elm, and her work colleagues had clubbed together to buy a wreath. It was a small, orderly possession.

Days passed, and still no sign of Blewitt. The police surmised that he would be local, bearing in mind that he had no job and money. Thus, he cannot have gone far. Rumours circulated that he had committed suicide. The police dragged all the local dams without success.

Mrs Blewitt's body was discovered on 17th June, so where had the prisoner been in all this time?

Police Constable Blackburn said he met the prisoner on the Dewsbury to Heckmondwike Road on 9th June at two-thirty am. He told the officer he had come from Morley, and he was a collier, seeking work. Joseph Brooks, a stoker at Elland Gasworks, spoke to Blewitt in the early morning of 11th June. He gave him food as he was starving. Mrs Elizabeth Lamb, who lived at Dunkirk Street Halifax, said the prisoner came to her house on 12th June and remained one night. She asked him if he was a married man, he replied, 'No, do I look like one?' she responded, 'yes. You are old enough to be one.' He had told her his name was Oliver Jackson. He removed his coat, and a razor fell from his pocket. The following day, he said to Mrs Lamb that he hadn't slept a wink. She checked his room. There were matchsticks strewn all over the floor, and there was a handkerchief on the floor with what she thought was blood on it. She thought it strange but said nothing.

Mrs Hannah Chapman witnessed that the prisoner lodged with her on 13th June. He told her he came from Leeds, and she asked him if he knew Beeston Hill. Blewitt said no, he came from the other side.

Blewitt secured work at Messrs Redman, Halifax. One of the employees had read about the Beeston murder in a Leeds paper. He mentioned it to Blewitt and asked him if he came from Leeds and if he knew about the murder at Beeston? Blewitt replied, 'No, I don't come from that quarter.' Then, not satisfied, the employee continued, 'but did you not read about it in the paper?'

'No, I'm not much of a scholar – I don't read much.'

The witness told him the Friday before his arrest. 'watch out. The police are after all those without moustaches.' Blewitt made no reply. John Boyles, blacksmith's stoker, had a similar conversation with Blewitt. Boyles became suspicious, so much so he gave information to the police. Detective William Bradley went to the Gasworks and saw the prisoner who told the officer his name was Oliver Jackson and came from Leeds. The detective then showed Blewitt the newspaper article. At this time, the prisoner admitted that his name was Charlie Blewitt. The detective charged him with the wilful murder of his wife. Blewitt made no reply.

Justice Ridley presided over Blewitt's trial on 4th August 1900 at Leeds Town Hall. As usual with a murder trial, there was a large attendance. Blewitt had an affinity with the ladies who, for some reason, found him extremely attractive. So when he came before the court, the Ladies Gallery was packed. Mr Bates for the prosecution opened the proceedings at some length detailing all the facts. He emphasised that police surgeon Dr Heald reported that the murder of the victim had, in his professional opinion, taken place whilst the victim was eating supper, most likely accompanied by her husband. The prisoner's mother, Mrs Jemima Bunney, told the court that she had made the pasty as a present for her son to take home to his wife for supper. At the time of her death, the pasty was half-eaten.

Furthermore, the amount of blood on the victim's clothes implies that the victim met her death where she sat. Also, the wounds on her hands indicating she would not have had the strength to cut her own throat and vice versa. If she had cut her own throat, then she would not have been able to self-inflict damage to her own hands. It is evident to the surgeon that these wounds occurred due to clutching a knife or a razor.

Neighbours came forward to give their evidence. Rodger Coffey no 8 Star Fold says he saw Mrs Blewitt around 8.30 pm, then twenty minutes later he saw Mr Blewitt. William Stanley 6 Star Fold again stated he saw the prisoner standing in the doorway of his house. Mrs Blewitt, he recalls, was cleaning her windows at the time, and he heard her say in an angry tone, 'I know better than that.' Although Mr Stanley did not know what Mrs Blewitt referred to, he added that he heard the victim shout at her husband a few weeks earlier, 'Get up and seek some work.'

John William Steel, a bootmaker, gave evidence that, in his opinion, the boots worm by the prisoner when arrested and the pair found in the house belonged to the same person. This evidence closed the case for the prosecution.

Mr Banks for the defence argued that if as had been suggested that Mrs Blewitt killed herself, she must have draped with the shawl over her head after her throat was cut and mutilated her wrist and thumb. It seems impossible that such a suicide would also coincide with her husband's departure from the house. The doctor had formed the opinion that this was indeed a homicide. Who else could have murdered this young woman except for her husband? There was ample evidence against him.

At this point, the prosecution pleaded with the jury on behalf of the prisoner. He commented on the absence of a motive – just why would the man want his wife dead? Charles Blewitt was of good character; and not known to the police. He loved his wife, but the couple was frustrated as he had recently been out of work, so he left home to seek employment. He did not kill his wife. He shaved his moustache off to appear younger so he would have more chance of finding a job. If he were guilty of anything, then he would have used a barber further afield and not a local one where he was known. The police found no weapon, and there was no sign of a struggle with evidence pointing to Mrs Blewitt committing suicide. Altogether this tragedy is nothing more than a case of suspicion. He asked the jury to hesitate and think carefully before pronouncing the doom of any man based on the evidence they had heard.

On the opposite side, the defence argued that if the jury discarded the theory, the victim committed suicide. Then who was the murderer? The last person to see her alive was her husband – but then he mysteriously disappeared – why did he do that? Mr Bates addresses the jury directing them to the facts of the case, and despite much of the evidence being circumstantial, he trusted that the jury would find the prisoner guilty.

In summing up, Mr Justice Ridley said it was for the jury to satisfy themselves to arrive at a guilty verdict. If it was a suicide, why was there no weapon found by the body and in reach of the victim's hand? Why was the door locked from the outside?

The jury must study the evidence and convince themselves of the facts and not by guesswork. Furthermore, they must be confident in their judgement that the murderer placed the shawl over her head after the murder. The jury was absent for 65 minutes. Finally, the foreman intimated that there was no possibility of the jury reaching an agreement on a verdict. Accordingly, the jury was dismissed, and the prisoner put back on trial with a new jury the following Tuesday.

Once more, Blewitt found himself on trial, and once again, the court was crowded, especially with women who flocked to see the prisoner's fate. Finally, after hearing all the evidence from both sides, the jury retired for 35 minutes and returned with a guilty verdict of wilful murder.

In the passing sentence of death, his Lordship assumed the black cap and said, 'Charles Oliver Blewitt, after a careful trial, the jury has found you guilty of the charge of wilful murder. I have only to say that I agree with the verdict. You will have the opportunity, which you have denied your victim of preparing for your great change. It only remains for me to pass a sentence of death.' Blewitt remained calm and unmoved by the judge's comments, and he walked calmly from the court back to his cell.

Many people objected to the verdict, and a  private petition sent to the Home Secretary. This appeal was unsuccessful, and Blewitt resigned himself to his inevitable fate, although he did continue to deny any involvement in the murder. Insouciantly declaring, 'Well, I suppose I should have to die some time or other, so it may as well be now – it doesn't bother me.'

Blewitt's execution day came on 1st September 1900. Several hundreds of people assembled in Armey Road all were waiting for the running up of the black flag to signal that the execution had taken place. Instead, after a restless night, Blewitt walked firmly to the scaffold, head held high, still denying his guilt.

Billington was the executioner, assisted by his son. Blewitt's death was instantaneous.

R.I.P Mary Anne Blewitt.

# CHAPTER 11

# 1904. Ganton – Nr Scarborough – Murder – A Terrible Poaching Affair.

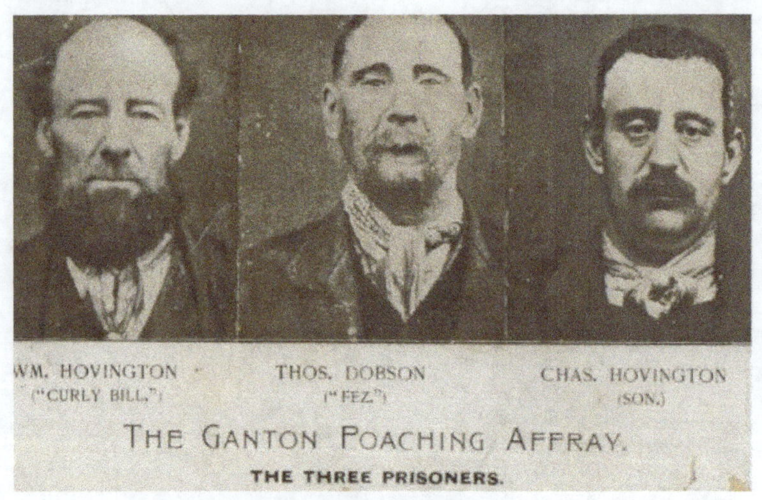



*© Author's collection.*

Ganton village, seven miles from Filey and nine and a half hours from Scarborough, has been associated with the Legard family for many years. The Legard's can trace a presence in Ganton back to the 1500s.

The first baronet was Sir John Legard (1631 – 1 July 1678), a landowner and a Member of Parliament.

In 1904 12th Baronet Sir Algernon Willoughby Legard (1842–1923) was the landowner of the Ganton estate. Well-known as it is today for its golf, Ganton's countryside is picturesque even in winter when the land is covered in a dreary mantle of snow. Amidst its beauty, Ganton The locals say that the pheasants are as tame as chickens. Like many other estates, poachers have had their share, and gamekeepers have taken all precautions to prevent them. This poaching problem was particularly true of the game on Legard's land, which he rented for shooting purposes to Mr Emerson Pickering of Garforth. Mr Pickering had planned for a big shoot on Saturday 26th November, and he had invited several friends to join him. It is a matter of conjecture about whether the poaching fraternity was aware of this, although it was assumed they were.

On the Friday evening before the shoot, gamekeepers Thomas Atkinson, Tom Gambles, Tom Morris, and George Wellburn, as a matter of precaution, had kept watch on the hillside between Ganton and Sherburn. All these gamekeepers were strong, sturdy men, well accustomed to rural life, as they had lived in the countryside all their lives.

They were trudging across the snow-covered fields at Potter Brompton when they heard gunfire between nine and ten in the evening. The gamekeepers knew instantly that the shots belonged to poachers. So they made their way to where they heard the shooting. As they approached the covers (small plantations amid a vast stretch of fields), they saw three men with guns. With the aid of the moonlight, they were able to make out three well-known poachers, Thomas (Fez) Dobson, aged 54. William Hovington, 59 and his son Charles Hovington aged 30.

The gamekeepers made chase, and a desperate pursuit followed. It is unclear precisely what the circumstances were, but finding the keepers gaining on them, one of the poachers turned and fired is unsure which poacher fired the shot. The shot struck Gambles in the leg and disabled him. Two of Lord Downe's gamekeepers joined in the chase from the adjoining estate together with another man. Once again, one of the poachers turned and fired their gun. The gamekeeper, Atkinson, fell. His face and chest riddled with pellet shots, evidentially fired at a short distance, whilst his already injured colleague Gambles received a shot in the lower part of his body. This action, it is stated, angered the keepers who raised their guns on the marauders, piercing their legs with pellets. Crippled and at bay, the poachers were now desperate and began to wield the butt end of their old-fashioned rifles on the heads of their pursuers with devastating effect.

Lord Downe's keeper, Weldon Morrison, received a nasty gash on the head, which put him out of action. His friends fared no better. The poachers managed to escape across the fields, and Gambles and Wellburn bravely followed. Again, the poachers turned and fired their guns; Gambles was shot in the groin and abdomen, Wellburn was on his own and desperate, appealing to the poachers' better side he pleaded with them, 'Go away lad's for god's sake, you have done plenty!' The poachers backed off, then came forward again when one of them heard shouting, 'let's finish him off!'

Scared, Wellburn lay on the grass and with all his strength and to save his own life, he fired his gun, shooting both the Hovington's in the legs. Wellburn's cries for help attracted another gamekeeper from Downe's estate called Caid. At this time, both parties used the butts of their guns, and Wellburn received a nasty gash to the head, and two of the poachers, the younger Hovington and 'Fez' Dobson, received severe scalp wounds.

Word of the affray soon reached Scarborough, to where the poachers would have fled. Detective Burrows and Constable Lyons were stationed at Stepney Hill Road when they noticed three men in a messy state coming down Racecourse Hill on their way into town. Knowing they had nowhere to run to, the poachers surrendered to the police. Most likely as they required medical assistance.

The gamekeepers were severely hurt, but the worst was Atkinson, a married man who lived in the village of Sherburn. He was taken in an exhausted state to his home, where his family called for medical assistance. Atkinson did not have the strength to say a word, he just lifted his arms, and he expired immediately. His colleagues, Gambles, aged thirty-four, a married man, and Thomas Morris, a single man, were taken to the Pigeon Pie Hotel at Sherburn. Gambles was in a terrible state and only half-conscious. The following day many visitors trekked to the village, all with a morbid fascination of catching a glimpse of where the events took place.

Dr Moriarty made a post-mortem of Atkinson's body. He found gunshot wounds to his neck and face and the upper part of his chest. Shots had penetrated the lungs, the artery in the heart had also penetrated.

Death caused because of internal bleeding from these wounds. Ganton was in mourning. Atkinson was local and from a well-respected family of cricketers and footballers.

Gambles and Morris continued to progress, but it would be a long time before Gambles was out of danger. Aged thirty-four, Gambles was from Ganton, a married man with four children. His injuries were severe. He was in a dangerous condition with gunshot wounds in the thigh and abdomen. Morris's injuries were not quite as serious. He had a scalp wound and severe damage to the eye. The doctor feared that he could lose his sight.

The funeral for Atkinson is one of the biggest funerals in the history of Sherburn. The church was only a few yards from Atkinson's house. Former school friends carried his coffin, the church was packed, and many tears were shed. A wreath arrived from Mr and Mrs Pickering, Atkinson's employer. The inscription read: 'In affectionate remembrance and with heartfelt sorrow at the untimely death of a faithful and valued servant'.

Sadly, Tom Atkinson's dog continued to sit outside the Greyhound Inn, patiently waiting for his master to return and would not be comforted. The poor animal just looked up and down the road. People remarked, 'There's poor Tom Atkinson's dog waiting for him.'

All the prisoners were powerfully built men. The elder man, William Hovington, had fifteen shots in his legs and two scalp wounds. The medical officer at Scarborough medically examined all before being transferred to Norton. Hovington's legs riddled with bullets. 'Fez' Dobson had two severe wounds on his head. The younger Hovington, Charles, was a member of the Imperial Yeomanry and had served in South Africa. When arrested, it was apparent that the three men had tried to remove all evidence of a struggle. Their heads were wet, and their handkerchiefs saturated with water.

All three men were taken into police custody at Norton and placed under lock and key in readiness for their appearance at the police court.

At ten o'clock the following morning, the three men were brought before the court and charged with night poaching and inflicting grievous bodily harm. All men made no reply. The police took into their possession the broken stocks of the guns believed to belong to the poachers. Evidence was recovered in the fields where the affray took place, with patches of blood visible through the trodden snow. The men were remanded, awaiting trial at York assizes.

The trial was heard on 15th March 1905 before Justice Ridley, for the defence was Mr Mellor. All three prisoners were well-known Scarborough men, and all were well-known to the police.

A man was dead and others seriously injured. This fact was not in dispute. The problem for the jury was to determine, if possible, who fired the shot that fatally killed the gamekeeper, Atkinson. Police regarded the elder Hovington as the perpetrator. If this were proved, then the Grand Jury could have only one duty: to return an actual bill against him of murder. At this moment in the proceedings, the judge declared that nothing he had seen would reduce the charge against Hovington Snr to manslaughter at that moment in time.

Regarding the other two prisoners, the question for the jury was whether they were a party to the act or just accomplices – if they were accomplices, then they too were liable in law with Hovington.

Hovington gave evidence; he said he heard one of the keepers say, 'give them a shot, you need to run – we know you'. After that, his son was shot. Up to that time, none of the three 'poachers' had fired any shots. 'We went about forty yards, then we heard the words, 'give the bastards another.' Then someone shot me in the leg. I do not know who fired the shot at Atkinson – none of us was firing any shots at the time!'

Cross-examined, he said he had carried his cartridges and powder in his pockets, but he threw them away as he had no use for them. Hovington concluded by saying, 'I did not see any man fall.'

Dobson gave evidence, stating that 'It was the big tall gamekeeper who fired the first shot, the one that hit young Charlie Hovington. I carry a single-barrelled shotgun, but I never fired it at all.' However, he did admit to using the butt of his gun over Morris's shoulder but not over his head.

After a lengthy summing up, the judge concluded that he anticipated that the jury should take the view that by a small margin, they could not beyond all reasonable doubt conclude a case of murder. They would find difficulties in determining who, if anybody, had fired the shot that killed Atkinson. Therefore the charge they must consider was a charge of manslaughter.

After a short period, the jury returned with a verdict of manslaughter against all three men.

His Lordship said he agreed with the jury's verdict, although he did think that the prisoners came remarkably close to the line of a murder conviction. 'It must be distinctly understood that whoever did load and shoot his pistol even at a distance, with the intent to cause grievous bodily harm, is guilty of murder.'

He, in his mind, was clear that it was not the keepers that fired the first shot – the prisoners did.

'Gangs of poachers – like these three men are a nuisance. They went out to poach and to resist authority, hoping to avoid capture. Unfortunately, on this occasion, they were unlucky.'

William Hovington and Thomas 'Fez' Dobson were both sentenced to ten years of penal servitude. The younger man, Charles Hovington, was sentenced to seven years of penal servitude.

A sentence of penal servitude usually included hard labourer. Following the Penal Servitude act of 1857, penalties were served in England, although the transportation of prisoners for longer sentences continued and was abolished entirely in 1868.

R.I.P Thomas Atkinson.

# CHAPTER 12

# 1909. Halifax. The Murder of Beatrice Cooke 'The Body on Shroggs Tip.

*Beatrice Cooke 1909. Credit Halifax Evening Courier.*

At 5 am Friday 22nd October 1909, an agitated young man walked into Harrison Road Police Station, Halifax and asked Sergeant Joseph Whittaker for a glass of water. He then told the officer that he wanted to give himself up as he had killed someone and thrown the body down Shroggs Tip.

The young man gave his name as Livingstone Thwaites, who lived at 15, Fairfield Terrace, Shroggs Road, Halifax. The sergeant deduced that the young man was worse for a drink, dazed and confused. The officer decided that something was wrong, but thinking it was simply the drink talking, said, 'Nonsense man, here have a drink of water then things will be clearer once you sober up, you'll see.'

'No, no, it won't,' sobbed Thwaites. 'I did it. I stabbed her in the neck with a knife, and then I kicked her down the tip. So I have, I've killed Beattie, she's on the rubbish. See!'

The sergeant had no choice but to take Thwaites' allegations seriously and investigate his claim of murder. The police remanded Twaites into custody pending investigations. The police searched the area and noticed signs of a scuffle along Snake Hill towards the tip. As you would expect, the area was covered in garbage. The refuge tip had a 40-foot slope to a hollow below. At the foot of the slope, they found the body of Beatrice Cook (known as Beatrice Smith), a twice-married woman currently separated from her present husband. Beatie's 'Merrie England' style hat was strewn on the ground along with her hatpins and a brooch which had the name Beatrice on it. Nearby, blood had run down the stream from where the body lay.

The police found a line of footprints down the slope of the tip. As if someone had approached the woman from behind. Footmarks were seen from the top of the tip, where it was apparent that an altercation had taken place. Consequently, the police charged Thwaites with murder.

Livingstone Thwaites was born at 21, Baker Street off Pellon Lane, Halifax, in January 1884, the youngest child of Thomas and Sarah Thwaites. Nine weeks before his birth, his father collapsed and died in front of his wife, leaving a large family in impoverished circumstances. Widowed Sarah moved the family to a smaller, more affordable house at 16 Pellon Lane, Halifax. Livingstone had trained as a taxi driver and as a journeyman painter. He joined the Worcester Regiment claiming to be one year older than he was. However, he was discharged in 1903 after receiving a conviction for a felony.

Before he gave himself up at the police station, Thwaites had called on both his brothers. He banged on his brother Walter's door, frantically shouting, 'I've killed Beattie, I've stabbed her in the neck and kicked her down the embankment by the tip.' He pleaded with his sister-in-law to believe him saying he would fetch the body back himself if they would take it in.

The couple were sceptical, not believing that Livingstone had killed anybody at all and that he was drunk and hallucinating.

Thwaites then went to see Thomas Jagger, his wife's stepfather, where he shouted at his bedroom window for him to come downstairs. Jagger couldn't make sense of his shouting and ramblings and took him inside, made him a cup of tea and fed him bread and butter. Thwaites took two rings and a pocketknife from his pocket and gave them to Jagger. Thwaites told him he had taken the rings off Beattie's fingers and asked Jagger to keep the rings as a keepsake for him. He said to him, 'here, take this penknife. This is the knife I did the job with.' Thwaites then said, 'The only woman I loved, and I have killed her – I'm going to give myself up.' He then walked away shouting, 'Goodbye, goodbye.'

Jagger was confused as he had no idea who Beattie was. He only knew that Thwaites was married to his stepdaughter, and she was not called Beattie.

Another neighbour named Bowers told police that he also saw Thwaites in the early hours of the morning. Thwaites had a cat on his shoulder, and he asked Bowers if he would look after the cat for him, as he was very fond of it and he was going away for a long time. Once again, the neighbour thought Thwaites was intoxicated and to appease him, he agreed to his request.

Thwaites had married Margaret Ann Thornton, known as Madge, in 1905. During their investigations, the police found a letter on a table at Thwaites' house addressed to Madge which said,

Dear Wife,
I have just realised what I have done. Forgive me. I ask of you. You see the dirty game I have played, but she asked me to do it. So, I did. I was caned up when I did it. Comfort dear mother – tell her I shan't fear anything, but I will face it like a man. I have put your lives in misery, but don't forget I am suffering now more than you can tell.

I hope, Madge, when you find another life partner, that he will be a gentleman. That is what you deserve. I was a fool, I can see that now, but it's too late. So, cheer up.

Love Thwaites  Goodbye.

The townsfolk gave every sympathy to Thwaites' wife. At twenty-eight, she was described as 'bright and vivacious' and married to Livingstone for almost five years. She described it as five years of misery. She was very apologetic for her husband's plight. She told her neighbours, 'he is okay when not in drink, but when in drink, he is evil! I keep my house clean; I work hard, I don't want to tremble to wait for my husband to come home from the pub scared to death as to what mood he will be in and if I will get a beating!'

Madge had a mark on her forehead where her husband had struck her following a drunken episode. Madge confirmed that she had scores of scars on her body inflicted by her husband whilst under the influence of drink. Five weeks after they married, he started to ill-treat her. She stayed with him as she didn't know what else to do.

Her husband went through bouts of not drinking, and Madge tried to keep him occupied by buying him chicken, fowls, and pigeons to tend to, which took his mind away from the urge to drink himself senseless. Thwaites was a painter by trade, and his work dried up in winter, so he had more time to drink, and then he neglected everything. Thwaites was so bad in drink throughout this time that she dreaded him coming home. She told the police, 'He would often take a knife to me – I was scared, once he had threatened me and chased me out of the house, Thwaites ran after me and was quicker and caught me, I screamed, but he struck me.'

She also told the officers that she didn't believe that he had committed the murder, as she considered that her husband was too frightened of losing his own life on the gallows to do anything of that sort.

'I didn't think he would do ought like that!'

Madge also believed that her husband thought the murdered woman was her; she had no suspicion that he was carrying on with another woman.

She knew he had been drinking all day, and Madge was under the impression that the woman latched on to him.

Following her husband's arrest, Madge was relieved, telling her family and neighbours that she was not 'overwhelmed with grief'. On the contrary, she considered it a 'lucky escape' from a different life of misery. She went as far as to say. God had spared her.

Thwaites was remanded in custody in Wakefield Jail, awaiting trial for the wilful murder of Beatrice Cooke. A few days after his arrest, Thwaites tried to commit suicide with a screwdriver on his throat and was found unconscious and diagnosed with ptomaine poisoning.

Thwaites strange behaviour was discussed at trial. Reports stated that on 14th December 1908, he jumped over a wall at the edge of a quarry and found unconscious on a ledge. He also attacked his brother during the night with a sword and needed to be held down. When he was 16, he managed to get hold of two revolvers, which had to be taken away from him. Afterwards, he was put to bed for two days in a delirious state. There was also evidence of insanity in his family. He had an uncle that had been in two asylums, his mother's aunt had been in an asylum, and his 4-year-old nephew was insane. However, Thwaites' medical report stated he was of sound mind and was not insane.

The trial started on 26th November 1909 at Leeds Assizes. Thwaites sauntered into the dock with his hands in his pockets. When asked how he pleaded to the charge of murder, he replied in a firm voice. 'Not Guilty.'

Many witnesses claimed they had seen the couple in various pubs around Halifax on the night of the murder. They were seen drinking in the Royal Hotel, Hall Street, the Lee Bridge Tavern and The Dusty Miller Inn. The couple left the Royal Hotel around ten minutes to eleven. The landlord recalled they were both in good spirits and were not drunk, but it was apparent they had been drinking, her on stout and him on beer. They were in fine fettle when they left and were singing 'Little clogs, little shawl'.

Beatrice's sister recalls Beatrice leaving the house around seven to go into town; she wore a fawn felt hat with a strawberry trim, a blue velvet jacket, and a black skirt. The poor woman found it difficult to answer any questions, sobbing that she loved her sister and had waited up for her, but she never came home, and now she would never see her again.

Another witness named Arthur Ratcliffe said he saw the couple walking up the road with their arms around each other. They were near Roukes Fish Shop when he overheard the man say to the woman, 'we will have a pennyworth in here,' the woman replied 'No' and refused to go in the chip shop. Instead, she told the man that she was going down Stannery Lane, whilst the man responded. 'You're not. You're going across to the tip with me.' The witness claimed that the woman tried to free herself from the man's grip – to no avail. Still, she walked towards the tip with the man singing as they went.

Thwaites' brother John gave evidence that his brother had not been the same since he had severe pneumonia when he was younger. 'He did strange things after that. Like jumping off chairs backwards and jumping into the quarry. He just wasn't right in the head sometimes.'

The prosecution argued that there was not the slightest doubt that Thwaites had committed this murder. After all, he had admitted to killing Beatrice at the police station. Yet now he has pleaded not guilty?

For the defence to argue that Thwaites was not guilty of murder, it must transpire that Thwaite was insane and did not know what he was doing when he slit Beatrice Cooke's throat from ear to ear. The jury must unequivocally have no reasonable doubt that this was the case. However, whilst in prison, Dr Benson Cook, the medical officer, observed the prisoner at Wakefield Gaol and found him quite capable and aware of his faculties. The doctor declared him perfectly sane, so in the community's interest and the protection of people, the only verdict the jury must give is that of wilful murder.

The jury deliberated for eighty minutes and returned with a guilty verdict with a strong recommendation for mercy.

His Lordship then passed a sentence of death, prefaced with the statement from the jury that he would forward their request to the proper quarter. As he left the dock, Thwaites cried, 'God help my family to stand it!'

Less than two weeks had passed when word came through that the Home Secretary had reprieved Thwaites' sentence of death to life in prison on the grounds of insanity.

Thwaites served his sentence at Parkhurst Prison on the Isle of Wight until 1916 when the authorities moved him to Rampton Hospital.

Whilst in prison, records show Thwaites' attitude to be sometimes cruel and often rude. Thwaite's family wrote to the authorities frequently requesting his release on compassionate grounds as Thwaite's mother was seriously ill. However, his wife Madge also wrote asking the authorities not to release her husband and be kept in jail as she would be in fear of her life if he were to be released.

Thwaites' mother died in 1919. A year later, Thwaites was released into the care of the Salvation Army in Essex, where he worked for a reformatory called 'The Land and Industry Colony' at Hadleigh.

A few years later, after being rehabilitated, he returned to the Halifax area, where he married Carrie Townsend. The couple were happy, lived together for many years and had several children.

Many people remember Livingstone Thwaites around Halifax town centre. He died in his hometown of Halifax in 1962, aged 78.

R.I.P Beatrice Cook (nee Smith).

*Livingstone Thwaites (National Archives)*

# CHAPTER 13

# 1912. Kimberworth, Rotherham 'Wee Little Children' The Double Murder of Frances Alice Nicholson & Amy Collinson (Nicholson)

*Kimberworth Rotherham Wiki Commons*

The evening of 15th November 1912 was a typical cold, damp winter's day. Ten-year-old Amy Collinson (Nicholson) and her seven-year-old cousin Frances Alice Nicholson were getting ready to attend the rehearsal for their school's Christmas nativity play. Both girls attended Meadowhall

School, Kimberworth, a small rural suburb two miles northwest of Rotherham. Nervous and excited, the girls were looking forward to taking part in the performance. Frances was incredibly excited as she had been given the role of a baby in the play, and she had to recite the verse 'wee little children to learn. She had spent weeks perfecting her lines.

Her birth mother, Hannah, was the unmarried sister of both her adopted mother Sarah and her cousin Frances's father, Isaac Nicholson. The older girl, Amy, was raised by her aunt and uncle, Arthur, and Sarah Collinson, whom she called mother and father. Her father was called William Beckett, but Amy had no contact with her paternal father.

The Collinson's had two other children, both boys. The family had recently moved from Wroot near Doncaster to take over the tenancy of Abdy Farm. Whilst just over half a mile away, the couple's brother-in-law, Isaac and his wife Dora had also taken over the occupancy of a cottage towards Scholes village, close to a local landmark, Keppel's column, a folly built on the Wentworth Estate, in a previously wooded area known as Scholes Wood or Scholes Coppice. The families were pleased that the children had family around as the girls were firm friends.

*Abdy Farm Inset Amy Collinson & Frances Nicholson.*
*© Illustrated London News.*

There was a shortcut from the back of the house across the fields, a lonely, desolate path that not many children or women come to that would care to walk at night. This path turns around by Binder's Farm into a road crossing the front of Collinson's cottage. Some way down the path. There is a shortcut across the field leading in a beeline to the back of the house.

Both parents had severe misgivings about the girls walking home alone at night in the dark, especially as there was a pond nearby, which the girls could easily fall into if they were not careful. Sarah Collinson's last words to Amy were:

'Will you be frightened?'

'No!' Amy replied. 'I have nothing to be frightened of!'

The younger girl, Frances, was not as confident; she was only seven and was especially afraid of walking home in the dark. However, her parents reassured her that she stayed close to her cousin Amy everything would be all right. The Collinson's also agreed to send their boys to meet the girl's part-way on the journey.

Reassured and full of excitement, the girls left Amy's house around 5.30 pm. Mrs Collinson still shouting strict orders to them as they left the house, 'don't forget you do not take the shortcut in the dark!' In 1912, the streets were unlit and smog-ridden, with plenty of dark places where crimes were hidden from sight and so committed with impunity.

The rehearsal finished around seven-thirty, and before the girls set out on their challenging walk home, they chatted and played with their friends Doris Wood, Emily Stainrod, and Ivy Broomhead. Not wanting the night to end, the two cousins went for a cup of tea and some bread and butter at Doris's house, where they confessed to their friend their fear of walking home alone. It was not until the girls had departed that Doris told her mother of her friends' apprehensions and Doris and her mother tried to find the girls, but it was too late. There was no sign of them.

Back at Abdy Farm, Arthur Collinson had arrived home from work at 7 pm. After his tea, he went to his shed to make a rabbit box. He finished making this at 8 pm, then sent it to his neighbour's house via his two nephews. (The boys were already at Abdy house.)

The plan was that Frances' brothers, William and Arthur, were to meet the girls and drop Amy at Abdy Farm, then escort Frances home to

Scholes. The distance they were to cover was around a mile or so, which should have taken them roughly 30 mins, allowing for dawdling, and gossiping with their friends. The girls were expected home by 9 pm.

It was getting late. The boys came back, but the girls could not be found. Amy's mother was anxious, she had expected them back before nine, and they had still not arrived.

Distressed, the parents walked down in the other direction to see if the girls had diverted along the route near the Grange Manor. When there was no sighting of the girls, the family proposed that the girls had most likely stayed over at a friend's house, which, although unplanned, wasn't unheard. The family hoped this was the case, and the girls were safe and sound with a friend. At 3 am the family gave up the search and went home, intending to find both girls the following day.

Arthur Collinson went to his work at 5 am, but his wife Sarah was frantic with worry, so as the rest of the family gathered with a few local neighbours to resume the search, Dora and Sarah went in a different direction. Not long after, Dora saw a hat which she immediately recognised as Amy's; Sarah's heart sank as she ran towards it. As the women got closer, they were stunned and alarmed at the sight that greeted them. Although she couldn't see their faces, she intuitively knew they had found the missing children. Both girls were lying in a ditch. Amy on her back with a protective arm around her younger cousin Frances, by her side. Their throats were cut, with their beautiful faces covered in blood. Sarah later said, 'They looked like sleeping angels.' The women's hysterical screams alerted farmworkers working on nearby land. The family rushed to the scene, and the police summoned immediately. What started as the disappearance of two young girls had now turned into one of the country's most diabolical double murder enquiries.

Immediately, the police started a search of the area. Detective Sergeant Brooks put together a team of police officers, who took a cast of an imprint they found in the mud. It looked as if somebody had knelt in a pair of close-weave trousers. Police also found a partial print of a boot covered with a boot protector, although the tread was indistinguishable, and a man's glove hanging from a tree.

Word soon spread about the close-knit community of the horrendous slayings of two innocent young girls. People began to flock to the area, making it impossible to preserve the crime scene. Reporters were soon on the scene wanting to be the first to report the story in their newspapers.

*The discovery of the bodies (marked with an X) Inset. The Nicholson's & The Collinson's. © Illustrated London News.*

What is puzzling is that the girls were murdered within 200 yards and within hearing distance of the Collinson's cottage. Yet nobody heard a sound. The girls were found distinctive and entirely off the regular footpath, but in a direct line and the shortest cut, the girls could have taken across the field. Furthermore, the back of the building was towards where the murders occurred, and the only entrance was from the front. The hedge was sparse and not able to hide the bodies of two young girls. So how did Arthur Collinson and his family, who had thoroughly searched the area earlier the previous evening, not found the girls sooner? Furthermore, when the boys crossed the field at around eight-thirty in the evening. They must have passed within a few yards of the scene of the murders. Which begs the question were the girls dead and lying under this unprotected hedge at this time? One of the boys was carrying a lantern, yet they saw nothing. Very strange!

The police secured the services of a bloodhound dog to assist them in tracing the murderer. After being given the scent from the glove the police discovered earlier, the dog picked it up and soon, the animal led police on a winding route for three miles until the early hours of the morning when they lost the scent. The dog regained the scent near a small wicket gate where police discovered a faint fingerprint covered in blood. The dog kept the smell for half a mile long before it was lost.

Doctor Robinson saw the bodies of the dead girls at 9 am. Both bodies were cold, and in his opinion, the girls had been dead for approximately 12 hours. Both had their throats cut from ear to ear. All the arteries and veins and the whole of the structures right through to the spinal column were severed. Death was instantaneous in both cases. There was a large quantity of blood on the ground and nothing to suggest a struggle. Following the post-mortem, and with horror and disbelief, the doctor discovered that ten-year-old Amy had also been raped. However, Dr Robinson considered that this violation occurred a few days before her murder. There were no signs of bruising on either child's limbs or bodies, and both girls were well-nourished and in good health. The doctor also confirmed that in his opinion, the girls died on the spot they were found, the bodies unmoved.

Bloodhounds were used to trace the perpetrator's movements to no avail. Although they found bloodstains on a wicker gate not far from the scene, the police decided this could have come from anyone, bearing in mind the number of people at the scene who had no doubt destroyed any scent trail for the dogs to follow.

The inquest into the murders opened on 19th November in the parade room at the police station conducted by the Borough Coroner, Mr WJ Bradford. As predicted, a large crowd gathered, hoping to gain admittance to witness the proceedings. Everybody was hoping that perhaps there would be some new evidence to throw light on the murder of these two defenceless young girls. On this occasion, the inquest adjourned till the following week.

A week later, on 26th November, the police took evidence from all parties. The evidence of rape against Amy was both graphic and brutal. Medical evidence was given by Dr Robinson, who said to the Chief

Constable that he would go as far as to say, 'that Amy was not outraged (raped) on the night she was murdered.'

With no further evidence to substantiate the rumours, the police continued their relentless enquiries, hoping they would soon bring the guilty man to justice. People of the town were scared and anxious about the possibility of a child murderer on the loose.

Rumours began to circulate in the town that Amy's stepfather Arthur Collinson murdered the girls. The consensus was that Arthur met the girls on that fateful night, and it was he who had violated Amy days before and had become scared in case Amy told anyone. He fit the police profile, and he had motive and opportunity. Arthur had the opportunity and knew exactly where the girls would be on their walk home and knew the best place to carry out this horrendous murder. The police questioned him, but it seems that he satisfied their line of questioning, and they released him without charge.

*Arthur Collinson and Isaac Nicholson.*
*Credit Illustrated London News.*

The funeral of the girls took place on 20th November 1912. Their tiny coffins were carried from each child's respective home and joined up after a short distance. The girls were buried at Kimberworth Churchyard side by side on a plot provided by the Churchwardens. Several schoolchildren followed the procession, and a crowd of around 12,000 people lined the streets to show their respects. The tramcar company put on extra cars just for the service, and thirty more police officers drafted to the area to keep order. Fortunately, there was no trouble from the large crowd. Shops and businesses closed, and the houses in the community drew their curtains in a mark of respect. After the service at the graveyard, the children sang the hymn 'O God our help in ages past. Around the graveside, a great many people. Primarily women, clustered in a horseshoe fashion around the space reserved for mourners around the graveside. Thousands of spectators surrounded the area hoping for a sight of the procession. People bowed their heads as the procession passed. But, the vicar said, 'the girls are now in the hands of God.'

The stress was all too much for Mrs Nicholson. She fainted at the scene and had to have helped from the churchyard.

The inscription on the girls' grave read. 'Amy Nicholson, Died November 16th aged ten years and eight months, and Frances Alice Nicholson Died 16th November 1912, aged seven years one month'.

As time went by, it seemed that there would be no arrest. The double murder of these two little girls is one of the most revolting in the annals of Rotherham's history. Nearby ponds emptied using a steam engine – to no avail – no weapon recovered. Scotland Yard sent down one of its most expert inspectors along with a sergeant. The police gave a reward of one hundred pounds for information leading to the conviction of the perpetrator. On Saturday 28th November 1912, a sensational development occurred. Vesey Hague discussed with a man, twenty-four-year-old unemployed showman's labourer Walter Sykes, in a public convenience in Kilnhurst. According to Hague, the conversation between them went, 'yon Bobby is watching me, watching me for the Kimberworth murders, and he is watching the right one, but he will never catch me. He will find me sharper than himself.'

Mindful of the one hundred pound reward money, Hague followed Sykes to Mexborough, where Hague gave all the information to the police. The police arrested Sykes and put him in the local lock-up, where he confessed to the crime. The Chief Constable responded to the telephone call informing him of the capture of the double-murderer with great relief. Aided by the police officers, Sykes put his statement in writing.

'Well, I may as well tell the truth. It is the first time I have mentioned it to anybody since I did it. I did 'em with a two-bladed penknife. I was drunk. I've sold the knife since. I am wearing the same clothes now, except for the trousers. I slept out that night, and I walked to Hemsworth the next day.' The police took Sykes to prison, but an hour later, he retracted his signed statement.

The prison doctor declared Sykes below-average intelligence. He was re-interviewed at seven the same evening, and he reaffirmed his involvement in the murders. This second statement was less explicit and did not explain why or when these brutal murders occurred. Sykes did not offer any further information. So, the police tried to trace additional details to give credence to Sykes' confession.

The physical evidence against him was weak — there was no blood splatter on any of his clothes. Sykes said he had thrown away the discarded trousers on Hemsworth Common as the local workhouse had given him a new pair. These were traced, but again, no blood found on them. The penknife he said he had sold was also traced to a man living in lodgings in Rotherham, Mr Herbert Hardy, who confirmed Sykes' story. However, this knife was only a single blade, yet Sykes was adamant that he had only ever owned one knife. So, police believed that he must have been mistaken when he said it had two blades. Incredibly, the rape of Amy was not investigated further, and there was no mention of Sykes involvement in that aspect of the crime.

The public had a divided opinion. Some were pleased that the police had done their job and apprehended the murderer. Some women felt safer knowing the perpetrator was behind bars awaiting his just deserts. Whilst others did not believe that the police had the right man. A letter appeared in the Sheffield Evening Telegraph, on 22/3/1913 which said,

*'Sir,*

*Is there any reasonable individual with any sense at all that could suggest that a man of weak intellect could have cleverly planned such a cruel deed without leaving more of himself than what was left in this case?*

*I know in a village-like Kimberworth, if the accused had either been seen in the district or its surroundings, someone would have suspected him before it came to this!*

*If he had been suspected, he would have been given into custody before he gave himself away. Again, I should like to ask if a drunken man can complete such a crime as this?*

*I do not think in my mind that he has ever been seen in the company with any child in Kimberworth at all, or someone would have noticed and suspected him before.*

*There are too many old inhabitants not to notice a stranger in the area, especially a man like the accused.*

*It can only be expected that a man of such weak intellect should confess that he had done it, as so many others have before him. What I say is that some persons or persons unknown should inter- est themselves in this case and start a petition for the culprit. I then believe that the actual murderer will be found, as I do not believe that the evidence is strong enough to hang a poor weak-minded friendless orphan like the accused.*

*We want to remember he is one of God's children and flesh and blood like ourselves. He needs our help, hoping someone will try to prevent this man from being hanged.'*

*Yours C.N. Kimberworth 20/3/1913*

Such a strong letter. Could it be that the writer was correct in their assumptions? Was it someone much closer to home who was effectively getting away with murder? The evidence against Sykes was weak. Sykes' employer could not account for Sykes' attendance at work in the days leading up to the murder. Sykes said he did turn up for work on 16th November, albeit extremely late in his defence. Amy's friends confirmed that they had seen Amy talking to Sykes three days before her murder, but this was not substantiated. The penknife with the double blade Sykes had sold but later recovered showed no traces of blood on the knife whatsoever. Sykes' trousers were shabby and much repaired, but again they showed no traces of blood. (Sykes later admitted that he had disposed of the original trousers in exchange for a new pair from   the workhouse.)

The case came to trial on 10<sup>th</sup> March 1914 at Leeds Assizes. Sykes stood in the dock fighting for his life. He pleaded not guilty after retracting his early written statement. Forty witnesses were called for the prosecution, some of whom said they recalled seeing Sykes in Kimberworth the week before the murders.

Around six-thirty in the evening, Sykes appeared in the witness box.

When asked if he had killed these two little girls, he replied, 'No Sir.' When asked if he was in Kimberworth around the time of the murders,

Sykes firmly stated, 'I have never been to Kimberworth in my life!' Sykes failed to convince the jury as to his movements on that fateful night. All he could say was that he had stayed in his lodgings. The prosecution deemed him untruthful, and due to Sykes' weak mind, they considered any further cross-examination in any additional capacity was futile.

Mr Hoare for the defence dwelt on the vain search for evidence of bloodstains and urged the jury to consider that the prisoner was of weak intellect and had perhaps got into this affair through his boastful remarks. He also stressed to the jury that the person who committed this horrendous murder would undoubtedly be covered in blood, yet not a single trace of blood was found on Sykes. There was no evidence to connect Sykes to this murder. The only evidence was Sykes confession which he later retracted.

His Lordship further expressed the opinion that apart from the confession, there was 'no case'.

The jury took just 6 minutes to return with a verdict. Guilty

The commissioner recorded a sentence of death.

Sykes hung his head when he heard the sentence and strolled away from the dock in shock.

The public launched an immediate appeal. Many were unconvinced that a man of such little intellect could carry out such a terrible double crime. Three weeks later, the appeal was dismissed. The response: 'the medical evidence showed that although Sykes was slow with his answers, he thoroughly understood what was said.'

The 23rd of April 1914 was the day of the execution. The tolling of the minute bell a few minutes after 9 o'clock was the only intimation that the execution was complete. Thomas William Pierpont and Albert Lamb were the executioners.

Only a small group of people gathered at the Wakefield Prison. Sykes walked from his condemned cell to the scaffold without any signs of trepidation. Doing his duty, Pierpont quickly pinioned him, and the execution carried out quickly. Before his death, Sykes nervously said, 'I am sorry.' Death was instantaneous.

Sykes left no confession; his demeanour remained calm and indifferent throughout his time in prison. Three of his aunts visited. He had no other relatives. *

With so little evidence against him, would Sykes have received the same conviction if sentenced today? Was Sykes capable of the cold-hearted vile deaths of these innocent girls? Why was the rape of Amy, which was such a pivotal part of the crime, not investigated further? Who did rape this innocent ten-year-old girl? Perhaps the perpetrator was much closer to home. Maybe one day, an appropriate body will re-examine this case, and the actual events of that fateful night will come out.

Let us hope so for Amy and Frances' sake. R.I.P.

# ABOUT THE AUTHOR

Wendy is a writer of both fiction and non-fiction. Her most recent books include Bloody Yorkshire Volume 1, Filey a History of the Town and its People, Scarborough a History of the Town and its People, Dr Pritchard the Poisoning Adulterer, Captain John Paul Jones & The Battle of the Bonhomme Richard. She is currently writing Bloody Yorkshire Volume 3. Wendy lives in Spain with her husband, two dogs and four cats.

* * *

If you enjoyed reading this book, please consider leaving a review on the vendor's website.

Thank you.

# RESOURCES

**1. ELIZABETH BOARDINGHAM & THOMAS AIKNEY**
Derby Mercury – 26/6/1767 Leeds Intelligencer – 26/3/1776 Leeds Intelligencer – 16/4/1776
Northampton Mercury – 1/4/1776 The Scots Magazine – 1/3/1776
Western Daily Press – 15/3/1909 Yorkshire Gazette – 12/3/1887
Anne Williams, burning at the stake for mariticide, 1753, Gloucester.
Illustration. Public Domain.

**2. MARY BATEMAN**
Chester Chronicle – 24/4/1809
Hull Advertiser & Exchange Gazette – 8/10/1809 Leeds Intelligencer
– 31/10/1808
Lancaster Gazette – 5/11/1808 The Scots Magazine – 1/12/1808
Illustration. Public Domain.

**3. JOHN SAGAR**
Leeds Intelligencer – 27/3/1858
Leeds Mercury – 1/3/1858, 18/3/1858, 4/11/1858 Morning Post
– 19/3/1858
Scarborough Mercury – 16/1/1858 Yorkshire Gazette – 20/3/1858

**4. THE PICKERING MURDERS**
Cheshire Observer – 3/5/1873 Chorley Guardian – 30/11/1872
Driffield Times – 23/11/1872 Exmouth Journal – 10/5/1873
Illustration-Illustrated Police News – 23 /30/11/1872

**5.  THE SHERBURN MURDERS**
Leeds Chronicle and Reporter – 19/10/1888 Leeds Mercury – 19/10/1888
Sheffield Evening Telegraph – 14/12/1888 Yorkshire Post & Leeds Intelligencer – 20/10/1888

**6.  HANNAH MOORHOUSE** Huddersfield Chronicle – 10/12/1881
Leeds Mercury – 8/12/1881
Shipley Times & Express – 10/12/1881

**7.  ESTHER NEALE**
Bradford Weekly Telegraph – 9/6/1888 Lancashire Evening Post – 4/6/1888 Manchester Courier – 5/6/1888
York Herald – 4/6/1888

**8.  EZEKIEL SUTCLIFFE**
Bradford Daily Telegraph – 25/8/1890 Hull Daily Mail – 26/8/1890
Leeds Mercury – 26/8/1890
Shipley Times & Express – 30/8/1890

**9.  SERGEANT WEEDY**
Leeds Mercury – 1/10 /1890 Yorkshire Evening Press – 30/9/1890
Yorkshire Herald – 20/5/1890

**10.  MARY ANN BLEWITT**
Daily Telegraph – 17/5/1890
Leeds Times – 17/5/1890, 30/8/1890
Yorkshire Post & Leeds Intelligencer – 13/14/5/1890

**11.  THE GANTON POACHING AFFAIR** Leeds Mercury – 7/12/1904, 16/3/1905 Sheffield Daily Telegraph – 1/12/1904 Western Times – 1/12/1904